GHOST
SHIP OF
DIAMOND
SHOALS

The Mystery of the *Carroll A. Deering*

GHOST SHIP OF

A Nonfiction Novel

DIAMOND SHOALS

BLAND SIMPSON

The University of North Carolina Press

Chapel Hill and London

Designed by Richard Hendel

Set in Cycles, Meta, and Flightcase types

by Eric M. Brooks

Manufactured in the United States of America

This book was published with the assistance
of the Blythe Family Fund of the University of
North Carolina Press.

The paper in this book meets the guidelines for
permanence and durability of the Committee on
Production Guidelines for Book Longevity of the
Council on Library Resources.

Library of Congress
Cataloging-in-Publication Data
Simpson, Bland.
Ghost ship of Diamond Shoals: the mystery of
the Carroll A. Deering / Bland Simpson.
    p. cm.
ISBN 0-8078-2749-5 (cloth: alk. paper)
1. Carroll A. Deering (Schooner) 2. Shipwrecks—
North Carolina. I. Title.
G530.C2979 S56   2002
917.56'175—dc21   2002004970

cloth 06 05 04 03 02   5 4 3 2 1

For Ann,

master mariner of my life

and Susannah, Hunter, and Cary,

our jaunty crew of children

The sea never changes and its works, for

all the talk of men, are wrapped in mystery.

Joseph Conrad, *Typhoon. Falk: A Reminiscence*, 1903

For all at last return to the sea—to Oceanus, the

ocean river, like the ever-flowing stream of time, the

beginning and the end.

Rachel Carson, *The Sea Around Us*, 1950

CONTENTS

1921

The sea is salty from the tears of women, say ancients and moderns alike, and who indeed can look upon any ocean from any coast in the world and not wonder at the great and moving being that has been the living end of so many souls? And wonder, too, of those upon some distant marge, some edge of the sea, some other where, who kept vigil for their overdue sailors and wept?

The time and the tides of over eighty years have now passed since to the roll of mystery ships that includes the *Flying Dutchman*, the *Patriot*, and the *Mary Celeste* was added the name of the schooner *Carroll A. Deering*. In a fog of unknowing, ships begat ships, and, in speaking or hearing of one of them, we spoke and heard of them all. In its day, the mystery of the *Carroll A. Deering* spurred the captain's daughter into an inspired investigation, and a nation and the best of her sleuths and maritime forces all followed her lead and worked to near distraction to discover what had happened one January night at Diamond Shoals.

The families of the shipbuilder and the captain and his crew all wonder still. This is the tale of the ghost ship that sails no more and yet lives forever sailing on to her grave, and of her phantom crew who in sailing her there passed into legend and so now can never die.

ONE THE SHOALS

JANUARY 31–LATE FEBRUARY 1921

WATCH

Cape Hatteras, North Carolina
Monday, January 31, 1921
6:30 A.M.

Off Carolina, where the great warm river of the Gulf Stream flirts with the cold southbound current from Labrador before spurning it and heading for open ocean, three great capes sculpted by the Stream's eddies ripple seaward and reach just beneath the waves for miles in shoal waters known the sailing world 'round and long called Frying Pan, Lookout, and Diamond. Over the sands of the Outer Banks this dawning long ago, billows of foam came rolling and boiling in. The fabric of the Atlantic Ocean's woof and warp unraveled and laid its bright strands out loose and shaking in airy, vaporous ropes that were nothing at all but oxygen, hydrogen, and salt, ocean spindrift strung out like white and ghostly hawsers from great mythic ships and flung in the wind all along the way of the wet, gravelly seabeaches from Cape Hatteras to Currituck. Yet more than spindrift was out there this morning, more too than the ever-threatening curl and pound of a disturbed and angry sea.

Just down the strand a ways from the black-and-white whorl of Hatteras Light, nearer to Cape Point and behind a white plank fence lay the U.S. Coast Guard's Cape Hatteras Station No. 183, a two-story cedar-shake building with gable ends, the tallest point for miles around except for the great lighthouse itself. Astride the roof's ridge sat a tall, square cupola with a pyramidal roof, two sets of doublehung windows constituting most of each wall.

From this lookout's perch Surfman C. P. Brady kept the 4:00–8:00 A.M. watch.

The winter wind was blowing ten to fifteen, and Brady heard it whistling lightly up under the eaves and around the cross-braces of the gables, watched in the dim but gathering morning light as it blew the tops off the waves cresting and breaking three hundred feet out. And all the while, in Brady's line of sight, the laughing, cawing gulls went flapping, circling, and wheeling by, at times hanging in place three or four akimbo, holding still in the cold air as if they had been placed or even painted there, and whether these avian forms that seemed more molded soot than bird were floating or flying, who could ever tell? He would see them for a few moments at a time, and then they would fade back into the smoky sky the way deer vanish into woods.

There was just now light enough for Brady to see all this, but the surfman dared not stare too long at those white spindrift lines on the seabeach, lest his tired eyes cross and get lost in a vanishing point in the mist and spray to the north. He rose from his post in the cupola of the cape station, climbed down the stairs to the mess for coffee—he had an hour and a half left on his watch. Regarding the jute bag of beans in the corner, the plantation name in Spanish faintly stenciled upon it and the shipping label still stitched into one of its rabbit ears, he then lifted a blue-speckled enamel pot from the small stove and poured scalding coffee into the blue tin cup with his initials on the bottom: C. P. B.

Then he made his way back up top, for he was the shepherd of Diamond Shoals, and they were his fields over which to watch by night. He closed his left eye and put his right to the small aperture at the near end of the station's great telescope, a prize possession of this outpost. Fully extended, the old glass, one of three the federal government had bought for use during the War of 1812, came to a length of seventy-one inches, and it took every bit of that power to allow one's eye to roam all over these twelve-mile shoals. Though Brady now stared out from the peak of his station, and this height gained him great range, still, as he slowly coursed the glass over Diamond Shoals he found he was mostly gazing out into the shoals's ever-shifting, heavy morning mist. There in the confine of the cupola Brady could feel the whole of the lifeboat building below him tremble before the wind, could feel it snap in a gust almost as a sail does when it fills fast. Almost as—

My God! Can you believe what you just saw?

Set the cup down, man. Rub your eyes, check yourself—nothing was there when you went below to the stove. Do you believe it now? You must, for the wind has parted the morning mists for real and there she stands before you, and you can only wish she were the apparition that she appears to be.

In the dawning mists, clouds of spray exploded from high, dark-gray rollers that marched in over the shoals and then rose and piled into each other and blew apart, and on these shoals most feared and dreaded by mariners the world over, there rose the five tall masts of a ship fully rigged with all sails set, a schooner upon the shoals—*up on* them—lodged and foundered. Whose hand was it that presented this craft to Surfman Brady, laying this enormous schooner into the mist-shroud of Diamond Shoals sometime during the long dark night?

Mother and lover of men, Brady thought, the *Sea*—see now what she brings. And sound now the alarm and shout the word, for wherever that ship hails from, she stands fast on the Outer Diamond. Say *the* word—shout it—the very worst word of the sea:

Shipwreck!

THE MEN WHO LIVED THERE THEN
Hatteras Island, North Carolina
Eighty to a hundred years ago

Shipwreck! How often it came as a cry in the night, or a howling against the wind at dawn.

A few handfuls, just clutches of men, set down every so often in stations along the sandy strand, were all that stood between the maritime pilgrims on a ship gone aground and death by drowning, pounding, or freezing—or all of these. The same waves that have beaten a boat from deep waters onto shoals will then beat her to pieces, and to the indifferent sea those persons aboard a craft in ruin are nothing more

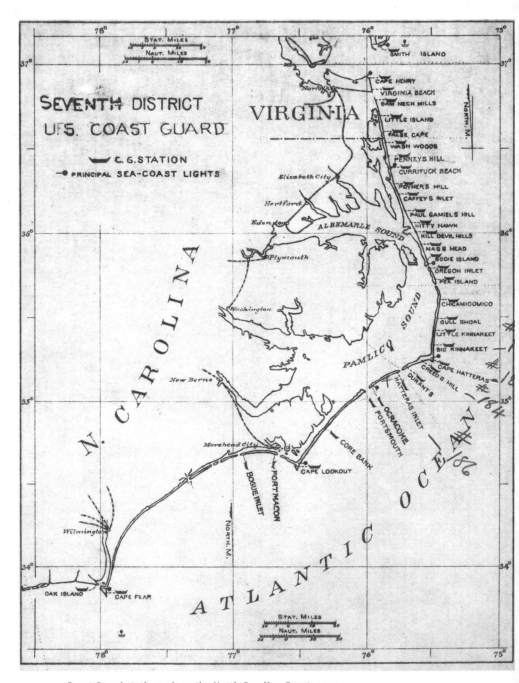

Coast Guard stations along the North Carolina Coast, 1921

than a few timbers to be rent and rendered into splinters, shreds, and flinders.

The men who lived there then, the lifesavers, were among the bravest in the world, and their names should be writ large. Writ upon *what*, though? The very sand they all but slept upon, as Hatteras was nothing more than a sandbar twenty miles out in the Atlantic? The ocean herself, for what was their life if not water? Like those who plied the sea, whose lives they were pledged to protect and, if called upon, to save, most of the surfmen's names are writ only in the ledgers that enrolled them in their trades. A couple of initials, a surname like Etheridge or Meekins or Midgett.

In awe and nothing less, sing of Rasmus Midgett who swam out and back and back again to the wreck of the barkentine *Priscilla*, one of seven ships that fell victim to the fabled San Ciriaco storm of August 1899, swam back through the still-raging surf ten times all told and single-handedly saved ten men from that wreck. And in awe and nothing less, sing too of his marvelous son John Allen Midgett, keeper of the station at Chicamacomico, who through fire on the waters led a rescue of the crew of the British tanker *Mirlo*, mined off Wimble Shoals during World War I, not even three years before this schooner that now foundered upon the Diamond.

Of course they would hurl themselves at the sea, and into it, for it was death's gauntlet and therefore the chance, the repeated chance, for the descendants of castaways to cheat death even as their forebears had, to cheat him of themselves and those afloat in the Atlantic shallows and seeking the grasp and safety of the shore so near. To go out into the roiling sea over which no human agency has ever held sway, or ever will, and save man woman and child, perhaps many, and have it be all in a day's work and worthy of a note—*assistance rendered, job well done*—and in so doing saving one's own life, necessarily and repeatedly, as a given part of that process, and have that be not noteworthy at all.

The job said they had to go out. Nothing on earth said they had to come back.

They were men enough to meet the sea and whatever pilgrims she tossed about and in her passion loved or merely trifled with—maybe

Cape Hatteras Station, U.S. Life-Saving Service, ca. 1900. After the Life-Saving Service and the Revenue-Cutter Service merged and formed the U.S. Coast Guard in 1915, this would become Cape Hatteras Coast Guard Station No. 183, and Surfman Baxter B. Miller, third from left, would be its keeper in early 1921.

shipboard, maybe overboard—and then set forth upon the seabeach, soaked and bedraggled and whether living or dead nothing to her, but to them who lived there then, everything.

A SURFBOAT AT CAPE HATTERAS

Cape Point
Cape Hatteras, North Carolina
Monday, January 31, 1921

So Surfman Brady, aloft at the station, and Surfman Gray, on foot patrol along the beach, both saw the schooner seemingly fixed out on Diamond Shoals. Brady immediately alerted the keeper of Cape Hatteras Coast Guard Station, Baxter B. Miller, who went up into the cupola himself and took a look of his own.

Keeper Miller was fearless hereabouts, a real son of the shoals. For helping rescue the entire crew of thirty-five from the German steamer *Brewster* when it foundered on the Outer Diamond in November '09, he had won a gold medal from the U.S. government and, from Germany, a silver watch inscribed with the Imperial Eagle. And he'd earned a silver medal two years later for saving the son of former Cape Hatteras keeper Benjamin Dailey when he was swept off the deck of his boat by heavy seas.

In the cupola now Baxter Miller cupped his left hand around the big telescope and pulled the shaft toward him with his right. With Surfman Brady's help for direction, he could see whenever the curtain opened for a second or two that miles away over the waters there lay a great schooner before them—now present, now disappearing, like a phantom, a specter, a will-o'-the-wisp, and he thought:

Smoky over the shoals.

Spectral she may have appeared, but she was real enough, too. At quarter past seven Miller telephoned the neighboring stations, Big Kinnakeet (No. 182), Creeds Hill (No. 184), and Hatteras Inlet (No. 186), to notify them and request they stand by for action. After another trip aloft, a second effort at reading or trying to read the truth of the moment through a veil of vapors, he telephoned those stations again at 7:30 A.M., telling each in turn:

"I am quite sure the schooner is aground on the southwest point of outer Diamond Shoals, and I am proceeding to the scene of the wreck."

First the Cape Hatteras surfmen, all slickered and sou'westered, stood by the long, white, lapstrake power-surfboat in the station, hands to the gunwales, and one of them threw open the big double doors. Once outside, they hitched the drayhorse, a tawny Belgian sixteen hands at least, to the caisson and Keeper Miller stood in the sharp, uprising bow and held the great horse's reins and down the ramp and into the sand seaward of the station they all went.

The gusting January wind blew spray and sand at them, and the damp sand gathered and caked upon the three-foot, wooden-spoked wheels, and the sea oats and grasses around them bent seaward, as the men and their boat slowly dragged through the dunes and over the

Transporting Coast Guard surfboat across beach, early twentieth century

open seabeach, the half-dozen men and the one beast drawing forward as if they next intended, like Poseidon of old, to plough the very sea itself. They had drilled weekly for this and knew this routine cold, yet they usually drilled on light days and not when the wind was blowing twenty from the west and freshening. The Belgian wore blinders—if the mare in her pulling and striving could have looked laterally and, instead of merely seeing the swath of gray-green-and-white boiling surf straight before her, could have seen how endless were her maritime fields, and how fierce and lathered they were this morning, the preposterousness of the vast work might have occurred to her and stopped her in her tracks.

There was neither stop nor pause, though. To the south hook of the cape the surfmen hauled the station's power boat, found the sea running very high, and thought perhaps it might be better for them to attempt to launch from the north side of the point. There, they found the sea ran even higher, so they returned to the south side, where now they were joined by the crews from Kinnakeet and Creeds Hill, the sea also being too rough for those men to launch from their stations farther north and farther southwest of the cape.

In the wet sand below the tideline the men halted and unhitched the front set of wheels from the boat carriage and led the mare forward into the shallow surf that was sheeting rapidly beneath them, till the wheels were clear and the front fell into the water and made a skid down which the boat would go, and then one of them walked the mare around and away, pulling now just the wheels, till she too was clear and unburdened and, standing alone and apart from the surfmen, looked away from them and their incomprehensible task.

This was a bold affair, but a humble one, too, this trying to put a vessel into the surf and get past the breakers and, in the parlance of the lifesavers' reports, "render assistance." Who awaited them out there on the outer Diamond in that great schooner? Who knew? But bring aid these men must—their mighty nation had placed them here at the edge of the world for just this purpose and no other. Of all the millions of people on the face of the earth, the only ones who might save that schooner's crew were these few surfmen, with their horse, their ropes and lines, and their very small craft.

Keeper Miller picked seven of the surfmen, along with boatswains C. R. Hooper of Big Kinnakeet and J. C. Gaskill of Creed's Hill, and these ten men, beginning at ten that Monday morning, threw themselves repeatedly into the roaring, boiling surf of Cape Point. The seas, coming hard, repulsed them any number of times before they succeeded, with both power and oars, in getting past the breakers and crossing the off bar and heading shoalward.

After a hard struggle the men had gotten to sea.

By 11:30 A.M. Miller's craft approached the scene of the shipwreck, but the angry and unpredictable shape of the seas—these shoals engendered great, high-rising, hollow-backed breakers the likes of which had slammed into each other since the first moments of time—kept them at a considerable distance from the huge schooner itself. As if it were nothing at all, the breakers out on the shoals flew about from

Launching Coast Guard surfboat, early twentieth century

every which way, crashing into each other and surging explosively to the heights of two- and three-story houses. Bos'n Hooper saw how the ship was driven high upon the shoals, lying in a boiling bed of breakers, and he thought with all sails standing she seemed to have been abandoned in a hurry. All the surfmen could see that the schooner's two boats were gone and the davit falls were hanging. They witnessed no movements, no signs of life on board, though they could come no closer to her than five hundred yards, not near enough to read through the breakers' spray and mist her name and home port. After several more attempts to move in on the distressed vessel, the Cape Hatteras surfboat came about and headed back in to the shore.

Men from the U.S. Navy's nearby radio-compass station had come down to the seashore to watch the Coast Guardsmen. The pharmacist's mate, the one they called Doc Folb, stood with the rest and thought, Look at her standing, sails all up, white and shiny way out yonder. Just look at her.

At 1:10 P.M., the surfmen returned, beached the boat at the south side of Cape Point, and Keeper Miller notified the Coast Guard's Seventh District superintendent and division commander of the results of his crew's efforts, which he then sat down and wrote out, longhand, in his *Record of the Miscellaneous Events of the Day*.

Nothing else they could do now, every one of them knew, until a larger craft arrived to help them out.

TELEGRAM TO HQ IN D.C.

U.S. Coast Guard, Seventh District Headquarters
Pasquotank River
Elizabeth City, North Carolina
Monday, January 31, 1921
4:33 P.M.

COAST GUARD WASHINGTON D.C.
UNKNOWN FIVE MASTED SCHOONER STRANDED DIAMOND
SHOALS SAILS SET BOATS GONE NO SIGNS OF LIFE SEA ROUGH STATIONS
NUMBER 183 184 186 UNABLE TO BOARD SCHOONER 1630
SEVENTH DIST.

WIRELESS

Fessenden, not Marconi now but Reginald L. *Fessenden* who had been Edison's top chemist, with his fifty-foot towers, one at Roanoke Island's north end and the other in Buxton at the broad bottom of Hatteras Island, here made wireless telegraphy into radio telephony. And it was not wisdom or truth or plain words of any sort, not the first sounds beyond telegraphic dots and dashes that he sent right through the air, over the Pamlico Sound waves and surf, over those waves and out of the absolute blue.

No, it was *music*. Three watts sending *music* fifty miles!

That breakthrough, that piercing of the very spirit of the wind, had come to Fessenden in Dare County on the Carolina coast in April 1902, and behind Fessenden's work out here in Dare was the old and mighty

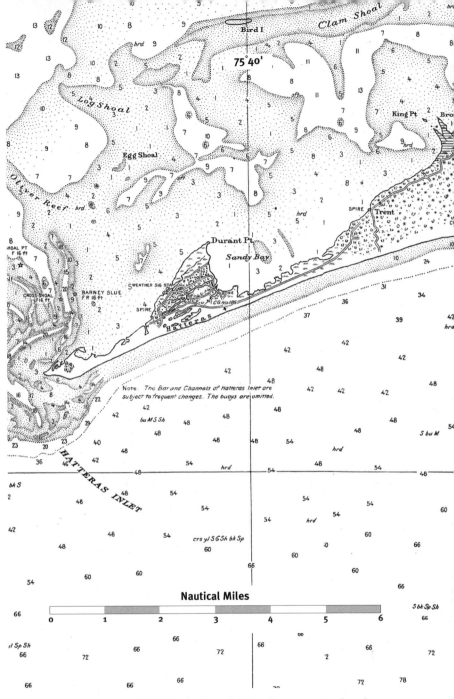

Cape Hatteras and Diamond Shoals. The *Carroll A. Deering* ran aground on the Outer Diamond at latitude 35°08'30"N, longitude 75°28'W (see circled area).

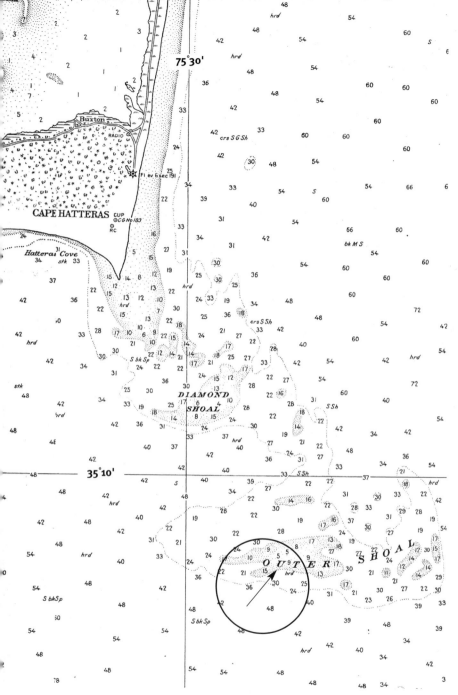

Detail from U.S. Coast and Geodetic Survey Coast Chart 1232, *Cape Hatteras: Wimble Shoals to Ocracoke Inlet,* January 1920.

question, symphonic even, all over again, and learning what he had done men and women asked it yet again in their hearts: *What hath God wrought?*

By the time of the Great War, the use of shipboard wireless was widespread, and so those who now wondered over the strange course of this schooner in '21 might well have asked another question, more particular and precise than symphonic, a quizzical air dancing upon the waves:

In this day and age, was there no wireless aboard that stranded ship?

THE CUTTER *SEMINOLE*

At noon on Monday, January 31, 1921, the Coast Guard's Norfolk Division wired its cutter *Seminole*, then moored at the Cape Fear River wharf in Wilmington, North Carolina. From the log of the *Seminole*: "12:00, received following telegram—Proceed to assist five masted schooner ashore near Diamond Shoals." Her succinct reply to Norfolk was: "Sailed for Hatteras 1355. *Seminole*.

She was a worthy craft for the task, the 188-foot, steel-hulled *Seminole*, built at Baltimore, Maryland, in 1900. Her beam was 29½ feet, her draft 11 feet 8 inches, and her displacement was 845 tons. *Seminole's* retrofitted boilers were only five years old, her hull had been repaired and improved, and she was judged by the Coast Guard to be in very good condition for a vessel her age. Wilmington was her home port, and her coastal patrol took her from Cape Hatteras to Charleston, South Carolina; she was armed with four rapid-fire six-pounders and fitted with a two-kilowatt wireless radio.

Keeper Miller's report made its course to the higher-ups in Norfolk by way of a relay from the Weather Bureau's station at Cape Henry, Virginia, and late Monday afternoon, Norfolk headquarters again wired the *Seminole*, now en route, and gave the cutter its first word of what to expect at Cape Hatteras: "Station crews report unable get within quarter mile of unknown schooner stranded southwest point Diamond Shoals No sign of life on board Schooner boat missing Inquire if crew is on lightship Obtain name of schooner."

U.S. Coast Guard cutter *Seminole*, home port Wilmington, N.C., on the Cape Fear River. Length 188', beam 29.5', draft 11'8", 845 tons.

Very early on Tuesday morning, February 1, the *Seminole* stood for Cape Lookout Light Vessel, passing her at 3 A.M., the lightship half a mile off the *Seminole*'s port beam, noted Lieutenant Commander C. H. Dench. At 8:45 A.M., she cut her main engine and drifted while the crew repaired the cutter's boiler feed pump, and soon the *Seminole* was under way again, by noon telegraphing Norfolk that she was seven miles southwest of the Diamond Shoals Light Vessel. Then at 2 P.M. she stood for Hatteras Lighthouse, passing a northbound schooner, and steamed into Hatteras Cove, where she stopped and at half past two signaled to the Cape Hatteras Coast Guard Station: "Can you send a boat?"

"Yes I can," replied the cape station.

"What has become of wreck?" asked the *Seminole*.

"Towed in by . . ."

"This last was evidently in error," logged Lieutenant Commander Dench, "as Hatteras Radio Station almost immediately advised that schooner in question was stranded on Diamond Shoals, with most of her sails set." The men of the *Seminole* then realized they had steamed right past the shipwrecked vessel and, because of her sails all being set, had mistaken her for a ship under way.

"Send a boat," the *Seminole* again requested.

"Boat is going to you," the cape station answered, and late that afternoon, at 5:35 P.M., Keeper Miller led his surfboat crew out to board *Seminole* and spend the night.

At a quarter till three, Lieutenant Commander Dench wrote that the *Seminole* was "anchored in Hatteras Cove in 6 fathoms with 30 fathoms port chain, Station 183 (Cape Hatteras) bearing NE ¾ E and Station 184 (Creeds Hill), NW × W ¼ W." A half an hour later, Dench wired Norfolk that he was sitting at anchor at Hatteras and further stated,

"Crew of schooner not on light vessel. Name unknown will attempt reaching wreck when sea abates."

Dench stood on the deck of his craft, regarding the thin island there before him, the longest of Carolina's barrier islands, an isolated and windswept fifty-mile strand of salt-sheared cedar and sea oats, gnarled oak and pine, with seven villages, seven Coast Guard stations, one lighthouse, and one navy radio and radio-compass station. Where the *Seminole* lay at anchor, one of the largest federal armadas of the Civil War had once lain in the early days of that conflict, waiting to bombard and blast the rebels out of Fort Hatteras down at Hatteras Village near the inlet. Twenty-five thousand troops had swarmed over Hatteras Island and its neighbor to the southwest, Ocracoke. But that was sixty years ago, and now there were only a few hundreds sparsely settled out here, many of them in the same government service as Dench; and, except for the all-black crew of the Pea Island station far to the north, all but one of the people living on Hatteras Island were white.

The wires were starting to cross, for *Seminole*'s last telegram—relayed through U.S. Naval Communications—would not reach Norfolk till just past eight that night. Meanwhile, Norfolk wanted to know—

wiring *Seminole* at 4 P.M. the same afternoon—if the cutter *Manning* might join the rescue effort. Again the navy relayed *Seminole*'s wire, the cutter answering at 5:15 P.M., "If sea abates *Manning* can assist, otherwise no," and at 7:19 P.M. came Norfolk's reply: "Send radio when *Manning* can assist period Report immediately condition of schooner and if any trace of crew."

At 10:30 Tuesday night the *Seminole* sent the report Norfolk would not see till the next morning: "No trace of crew schooner stranded about center of outer shoal apparently not badly damaged and all sail set unable approach closer than one mile in present sea As seas are breaking over her at present but not breaking up."

AN OFF-NOTE FROM THE JERSEY SHORE

Atlantic City, New Jersey
Tuesday, February 1, 1921

Coast Guardsmen watching the Atlantic coast around Absecon Light at two in the morning saw "a vivid flash of light at sea, followed by an explosion." Surfman Norris Smith of the South Brigantine station was surprised by this flood of light, which illuminated a calm sea over a very wide area. Then followed the long low roll of what he took for an explosion. Smith held his night glass trained on the spot whence came the great light, but there was no repetition of it.

Similar reports came from the Little Beach station twenty miles up the coast, as well as from the inlet patrol, and naturally the Coast Guardsmen wondered whether or not a vessel had blown up. Power boats put to sea at once but found no trace of wreckage, nor saw any signals of distress.

At dawn Captain Allen flew from the inlet in a Curtiss seaplane, went thirty miles straight out to sea and then climbed to 5,000 feet, using binoculars and combing the sea and shore for hours, but his search was fruitless.

For days both naval and amateur radio operators along the Jersey coast would keep their receivers up and open, all of them hoping to detect any distress call that might come through, or for some word from a sulfur steamer that had sailed from Sabine, Texas, about January 20, bound for Portland, Maine, the now-missing *S. S. Hewitt*.

But no word came, nothing washed ashore, and nothing was ever recovered.

WHERE AND WHY? THE WORKING PRESS WONDERS

Something *all* Norfolk would see the morning of the 2nd of February was splashed across the front page of the *Ledger Dispatch*: Ship Is Abandoned; Crew Is Missing; ALL SAILS ON SCHOONER ARE SET; Coast Guardsmen Still Can't Get Near Enough to Make Out Name.

"Where is the crew of the strange schooner wallowing helplessly in the seas off Diamond Shoals?" the morning paper asked.

"Why was the vessel deserted with all sails set?

"A Coast Guard crew that has been frantically trying for two days to reach the strange ship, whose name is still a mystery, are puzzled by the peculiar circumstances under which the vessel was abandoned."

THE CUTTER *SEMINOLE*
Diamond Shoals, North Carolina
Wednesday, February 2, 1921

Seas ran heavy in the morning, the weather rainy and misty with a moderate northeast breeze. The Cape Hatteras surfboat boys who had spent the night shipboard took off from the cutter *Seminole* to see if they could get any closer to the wreck today than they'd been able to so far. But the crew of Station No. 183 was rebuffed yet again by the great waves and again had to give it up. The sailors on the cutter bade them godspeed and stood on deck and watched them as they made their way back to shore.

Having wired at noon a report to Norfolk from Hatteras Cove that the schooner was in the same condition today as yesterday and that there were strong northeasterly winds and heavy seas, Lieutenant Commander Dench, who hailed from the little Detroit riverport of Wyandotte, Michigan, headed on out around the shoals when the weather cleared a bit in early afternoon. At a quarter till three this winter's day, he found himself steering his command north by east half east toward the mysterious stranded schooner. He took soundings at regular intervals, and, as he logged, "kept the lead going when close to the shoals." Just before 3:30 P.M., he backed the *Seminole* to within three-quarters of a mile of the ship, stopping in six-and-a-half fathoms.

"The surf was running high over the shoals," he wrote, "and occasionally breaking over schooner's poop. It was impossible to read her name but it appeared to be a long one, and the home port looked to be Bath, Me., however this could not be positively made out." Nowhere on the ship could he discern any sign of life. He declared the schooner "a vessel of about 3500 tons, painted light gray or white, with a black stern. Practically all her sails are set except the flying jib. She lies pointed about N × W and on the S. Side of the outer shoal in about 35 degrees 08'30" North, 75 degrees 28' West. She was not pounding so far as could be seen, and she is staunch as yet. No wreckage alongside of her was seen. She is listed to starboard 4 or 5 degrees."

Though her hull, masts, and sails seemed intact to Dench, even so, seas were breaking over her. How much more could she stand?

And how much could *he*? A few minutes later, Dench steamed southwest (3:35 P.M.), then turned west-northwest (3:47 P.M.), and at 4 P.M. sailed for Cape Hatteras Lighthouse on a bearing of N × E ¼ E, the beacon being then about eight-and-a-half miles away. Having been thwarted by Diamond Shoals, even failing to gain a positive identification of the vessel, and with his boilers now badly salted and his condenser leaking, with the whole mess acting up and deviling him again, Lieutenant Commander Dench came about.

The *Seminole* left the scene at 4:45 P.M. and stood for her home port, for the Cape Fear River and Wilmington's wharves.

LULA WORMELL

57 Lawn Avenue
Portland, Maine
Wednesday, February 2, 1921

Overdue?

"Why, Mother," I said when she told me, "what's that but a word? A little late, that's all, Father's ship is just a little late."

I lived in the house next door to Father's and Mother's place on Lawn, and she always came over and passed the time around here when he was away at sea. So she was the one who met the man at the door, and maybe she saw something in his eyes, his face, when he gave her the report from the shipping agents. Maybe she saw a little cloud that I couldn't yet see, or wouldn't. So I didn't argue with her.

"I'm going in the parlor to sit down for awhile," she said, shaking her head no when I asked her if she'd like tea.

As if nothing were wrong I lit the back burner and put the copper kettle on it, the one with the rattaan handle so you don't need a pot-holder. And I waited.

You want to keep busy, keep your hands occupied, when you feel your nerves slipping away from you, a little unraveling coming on. From the drawer next to the sink, where we kept the scissors and can opener, the whetstone and all of that, I fetched the teaball and dipped it into the special tin with the little twigs of dark, pungent tea inside and packed it tight and watched the blue flames lick the copper bottom of the pot.

Tea all the way from China, Father'd said when he came home with it last year. Of course, he didn't bring it all that long way, but he *might* have. For he's been all around the world and Lord knows he knows the way. A deep golden-colored tin, with Chinese figures all over it like some kind of dancing code—so mysterious, to us anyway, though a child over there could read it at a glance and take it all in, while I could sit here in this kitchen in Maine and stare at it the rest of my life and never know boo.

Well. Some things are lost in this world but most things aren't, so don't think about it, I kept telling myself. Or else Father's ship will be like the watched pot here that never boils, and she'll be always overdue, and where would—

Oh, there's the whistle, now!

THE CUTTER *MANNING*, THE WRECKER *RESCUE*
Diamond Shoals, North Carolina
Friday morning, February 4, 1921
10:20 A.M.

Two ships—the Coast Guard's cutter *Manning*, a 205-foot, 1,150-ton veteran of both the Spanish-American War and the Great War just past, along with the salvage company's tug *Rescue*—had plied down from Norfolk on Thursday the 3rd. As they did, a man from the Associated Press wire service got aboard a Hatterasman's fishing boat and visited the shipwreck, which was then resting easy in a subsided sea.

The *Manning* anchored off Diamond Shoals lightship, and the *Rescue* reached her about 9:30 A.M. on Friday, and then together they approached the schooner in a relative calm Friday morning. To all the hails and halloes from the Coast Guard no answer returned, so the *Manning* stood back and let *Rescue*'s Captain James Carlson, agent for the well-known Merritt and Chapman Derrick and Wrecking Company, approach the great sailing craft that—though they had come to float her if they could—now seemed fixed to the Outer Diamond as if she had grown there, or been planted there by the hand of God.

Now they could read her nameplate, and they confirmed the word sent out midafternoon the day before by the wire-service man to the Weather Bureau at Cape Henry, and all doubt as to her identity evaporated—the massive schooner, over 250 feet stem to stern, was the very one some days overdue at Hampton Roads, Virginia:

She was the *Carroll A. Deering* of Bath, Maine.

In the *Rescue*'s yawl boat, Captain Carlson left the tug, and he and four of his men—engineer Olsen, wrecker foreman Samuelson, and wreckers George Snow and Angelo Real—motored to the schooner's port-side bow, the lee side, and with some trouble boarded her by climbing a rope that was hanging over, a task that would have been deadly, impossible any time in the preceding four days. The schooner, from the continuous pounding she took and from all the wind in her sails, had so wedged herself down into the sands of Diamond Shoals that her deck was now no more than six feet above the *Rescue*'s boat, which floated in only eight feet of water!

She is too grand for such a fate, thought this new and momentary master on the deck of his ruined command, but this indeed is what she gets.

The schooner's deck undulated like a serpent, the seas breaking over her and water washing into the hold through windows and skylights and companionways. Carlson beheld a marvel, a ship whose stem and stern had been so twisted by several days in the waves that now she seemed to be simultaneously rolling in opposite directions. Carlson knew as soon as he saw how low she rode in the seas and how the seas filled her hold that she would never rise from this fix, not as anything more than a derelict, anyhow.

Only the flying jib was not set, and the wind had already blown out and shredded two topsails. The *Deering*'s two large anchors were lost, along with one of her chains; on her second chain was a smaller kedge anchor, shackled in regular fashion and triced up with rope, hauled up well out of the water close to the forecastle head. By sounding, Carlson judged the ship's keel to be buried as much as fourteen feet deep in the sands of Diamond Shoals, found oceanwater in the hold level with the sea outside and within five feet of the upper deck, and saw that the midship halyards were out of place and had washed about loose in the seas.

Carlson and his wreckers did not go below into the lazarette between decks but only looked down into it, seeing some barrels, some ropes, and sails all wet. They removed nothing.

The *Deering*'s forecastle was built partly above and partly below deck, the crew's quarters being portside, the engine room and engineer's quarters starboard, several steps down. Inspecting it, Carlson found the forecastle just about bare.

Someone had been fixing to eat. In the galley amidships lay a pot of pea soup, a pan with slabs of spareribs in it, and, on one burner of the stove, a pot of coffee.

But see here, thought Carlson as he wandered aft: Why was the steering gear ruined, the wheel itself broken, the binnacle box bashed in and shattered and a nine-pound sledgehammer nearby (to repair, or to destroy?), the rudder disengaged fifteen feet from its stock and the stock now slammed up through the deck? He couldn't say whether the steering gear had been wrecked before the *Deering* struck the shoals, or after. The soup and meat slab and coffee he had seen all made sense, but what sort of diet was all this?

The *Deering*'s two boats—she had carried a common dory and a twenty-four-foot ship's yawl, equipped with a two-cylinder, six-horse-power Mianus motor—floated elsewhere or not at all. They were no longer with the ship. During the abandonment, the crew had simply sliced the boat falls, and both davits and falls were way out over the stern. The sidelights, the red and green running lights, were burned out, as were two red lights high aloft, signals of a ship in danger that no one anywhere had seen—unusual, thought Carlson, for all four of these lights to be up at the same time.

Aft, beneath the quarterdeck, Captain Wormell's cabin had but a few clothes strewn about in it, his bed was unmade (the bedding wet from the seas that had washed into the cabin), and the spare room gave Carlson the impression that it may have been occupied; curiously enough, the captain's trunk and grip and large canvas bag were gone. Upon a table in the chartroom lay the ocean chart, spread out. On the floor of a small side room, two or three pairs of rubber boots lay scattered carelessly about.

Yet where were the ship's nautical instruments, her chronometer? Her papers? Her log?

From the *Deering* that Friday, all that the *Rescue*'s men salvaged were one foresail, one mizzen sail, two jibs, an American flag, a Union Jack, twenty-two code flags, three cabin chairs, a lounge, two sidelights, two riding lights, one red light, and one bell. Foreman Samuelson picked up Captain Wormell's Bible and carried it to Carlson, who would send it to the captain's family. In another small act of kindness, Carlson saved three nearly starved cats and took them back to the *Rescue*'s steward, L. K. Smith, who adopted them.

No captain. No crew. Just a trio of ship's cats found and accounted for.

Some men and women read texts, books, and newspapers only; some read the tracks of animals—or men—in pathless barrens of the lowlands and remote laurel hells in the high blue hills; some read the soil, the lay of the land, for what it might grow and what its contours might hold fast, or loose; and still others read the skies, for weather, for omens, for hints of what may be in time future or what was in time long lost. James Carlson's skill, his very lot in life, lay in assaying all manner of craft in wrack and ruin and finding reason and meaning and value in remnants there, and if fortunes can be read in the palms of men and women, or in their eyes, or even in the small furled missives the Chinese enfold and cook within thin sweet crusts, then fortune too presented herself to be read without embellishment on such a deck as Captain Carlson now strode.

And what he read, what he heard in the salt-spray wind, was a series of simple questions that the odd scene of the unpeopled ship put to him, as well as the queries the very oak and pine, the rope and wires and canvas and spars, all in one sang to him in a moaning refrain:

Am I worthy?

If I am not, can I be made so again?

How came I to this end?

LULA WORMELL

57 Lawn Avenue
Portland, Maine
Friday, February 4, 1921
4:30 P.M.

From the front bay window I stood watching, looking out, and so happened to see that towheaded boy not yet thirteen roll his bicycle up to the front gate of my big house in Portland. Letting it fall against the iron-fence pickets, he then rushed through the gate and came running up six steps to the porch and pounded with his hand upon our dark, heavy front door. When I opened it, I regarded the boy solemnly for a few moments and must have frightened him, for he backed up a full step as if he were withdrawing in fear of me.

Did I already know why he'd come? Didn't I? I reached proprietarily for the yellow envelope in his left hand, as if it were mine. The Western Union boys usually thrust their missives proudly forward, but this one just let me pull it from his grasp, like he had forgotten what to do, or why he was even there on Lawn Avenue.

"Who is it, Lula?" my mother called from the kitchen back down the hall, but I did not answer.

Instead I stepped onto the front porch, shutting the door quickly behind me—it was February and nearly sundown and there was a cold wind off the sea, after all—and tugging at the narrow strip of the envelope's flap that secured it. Now the boy smiled at me—but why? Did he think that this was a message from a beau somewhere, a sailor maybe, telling me he would be in Portland soon maybe, or maybe asking me to join him way off in the Berkshires maybe, and elope?

Oh, my, how I have remembered that boy. She will smile at me in a second, just another second, he must have thought, believing himself to be, if not Cupid, at least a Mercury bearing romance.

But I did not smile. I raised my head and gazed from the small yellow paper to the boy's happy and expectant face, and felt my eyes well up with tears. Boy, do you know how wrong you are? My sailor will not be in Portland soon—nor will there be any elopement, nor any romantic assignation, for he is my father.

"Go."

"I can wait for a reply," he said, reaching into his coat pocket and bringing forth a little tablet. "I can write it for—"

"Go!" I truly croaked that order at him, and he ran from me, stumbling on the lowest stair, catching himself, glancing up at me as he lifted his cycle away from the fence, wondering (I suppose) what was wrong with the telegram's message, what in those few moments he might have done wrong himself. He was escaping something, though he didn't know what. Fifty yards down Lawn Avenue he was, by the time I had read the paper again, and as I called after him "I'm sorry!" he disappeared around the chestnut tree at the corner, and must not have heard.

I am the captain's daughter, and the telegram the boy from Western Union brought had begged to inform Mother and me that there were "no signs of life" upon the ship, for five days now hard aground far to the south upon Diamond Shoals, and that it was now in fact confirmed this morning by the United States Coast Guard to be the schooner *Carroll A. Deering*, my father's craft.

WORD GETS TO THE KENNEBEC

226 Washington Avenue
Bath, Maine
February 5, 1921

The G. G. Deering Company, builders and managing owners of the *Carroll A. Deering*, opened Saturday and awaited further word from co-owner William Merritt, the ship's original captain, who had left Maine Wednesday for Norfolk and arrived there yesterday.

Captain Merritt's night-letter showed up first thing—by dark Friday, there was still no trace of the *Deering*'s captain and crew.

His telegram about the *Deering* herself reached the firm Saturday afternoon. It would be impossible, wired Captain Merritt, to save the vessel.

LULA WORMELL

57 Lawn Avenue
Portland, Maine
February 7, 1921

Could there have been a collision? Mama and I wonder. Some piling into each other of the *Deering* and another craft, possibly the sulfur steamship *Hewitt* that we've heard was northbound that night, and in the very same waters as Father?

If the *Hewitt* struck the *Deering* in the darkness, that may have been cause enough for the *Deering*'s men to abandon ship and go aboard the *Hewitt*—yes, it could've happened that way.

This mystery is nearly driving us wild—there's so much we need to find out, and, though my eyes are like a kestrel's on the papers, everything is so uncertain and unclear. Why, there were nine men from Portland in the *Hewitt*'s big crew—and there may've been as many as fifteen! If we find them, will we also find Father and his crew?

Will we?

Who can know anything at all for sure?

W. O. SAUNDERS

Offices of the Independent
505 East Fearing Street
Elizabeth City, North Carolina
February 12, 1921

Been *some* couple of weeks in Betsy Town, I tell you what.

First shad of the season came in—William Tillett down at Big Flatty Creek caught them—couple of four-pound bucks and one five-pound roe-fish. Our fish dealers on the Pasquotank are really gearing up, buying here and selling to the Dock Street Fish Market in Philadelphia. Late March, if the wind pushes enough salt water into the sound, why, those Stumpy Point boys'll be just hauling them in. And we'll be shipping shad out of here by the boxcar load.

Monday the 31st they had a Toonerville comedy playing at the Alkrama Theater—"Skipper's Narrow Escape"—and then Friday they were showing "The Veiled Mystery." Missed em both—people don't pay a newsman to go sit in the movies.

And speaking of news, guess you heard about Mrs. Vanderbilt's speech.

Mrs. George Washington Vanderbilt—heiress to her late husband's rail and shipping fortunes, as well as to that little western Carolina chateau, that overblown cottage he called Biltmore—was just talking to the North Carolina General Assembly, met in joint session in Raleigh to hear whatever she, as the new chairwoman of the State Fair, might have to say.

"I don't know much about speeches," Mrs. Vanderbilt told the honorables, "but I do know that a speech should be like a skirt: long enough to cover the subject but short enough to attract attention." The legislature flat loved her, applauded her brief remarks long and hard.

Well, the way I see it, just *being* Mrs. Vanderbilt enables her to attract attention, skirt or *no* skirt.

THE LOCAL SALVORS
Diamond Shoals, North Carolina
February 14, 1921

On Valentine's Day, four small sailboats went out to the shipwrecked *Deering* from Hatteras, and these fifteen men boarded her: Elmer Stowe, Millard Stowe, Rube Stowe, Walter Stowe, J. I. Willis, Roscoe Burrus Jr., J. I. Stowe, Sam Stowe, Norwood O'Neal, Tyne Willis, Phil Austin, Roscoe Burrus Sr., B. F. Stowe, Fred Stowe, and Lon O'Neal.

They sailed out to her thinking their boats would not be able to carry back with them all the new rope that should have been on the *Deering*. And though they hardly returned to Hatteras Village emptyhanded, still, when they got upon her and looked over the strewnabout and unkempt messes in the fo'c'sle and the captain's cabin alike, they all had but one thought and one thought alike:

She had already been plundered.

VENDUE
Hatteras, North Carolina
February 23, 1921

Everything Carlson and the *Rescue* wreckers had left aboard the *Deering*—and that the local boys from Hatteras Island had subsequently retrieved—now went on public sale at Hatteras Village, under the authority of W. L. Gaskill, wreck commissioner.

First went the food: small quantities of beef, pork, ham, and bacon, of coffee and curry, peas, beans, pepper, and salmon, of mustard, yeast, hops, and tapioca, and of grits, pumpkins, tomatoes, peppers, molasses, mutton, milk, prunes, and lard. Most of it sold for anywhere from a nickel to ninety cents, though the ship's sugar brought three dollars, her flour five and a half. The buyers—all of them living between Buxton and Ocracoke—paid $44.05 for the *Deering*'s groceries.

Furnishings out here at the edge of the sea were harder to come by than food, and these the bidding public valued much more highly. A table sold for $12.00, a chiffonier for $13.50, a set of chairs for $14.50, and a bedstead for $22.50. Lanterns went for two bits, though lamps got as high as $2.25. Eight mattresses were brought forth; Annie Austin made off with two for $1.75, but Irish Willis paid $12.00 for his. Brooms, buckets, doors, tables, pillows, blankets, linoleum, hoses, boxes, twine—everything must go! More than one of the six single-spaced legal pages listing the *Deering*'s items was devoted to "rope." C. B. Foster paid $19.00 for his rope, but Commissioner Gaskill only paid a dime for his.

Irving Stowe bought some nautical charts for a quarter. J. C. Gaskill of the Creed's Hill Coast Guard station got the captain's trunk for $5.00, and A. J. Gray got his desk for $35.00.

The wrecked ship was sold to Lee Robinson for $25.00.

The total for material and food taken off the ship came to $841.75, less the wreck commissioner's 5 percent, less the cost of a watchman and advertising ($25.67), and then less the salvors' 60 percent—leaving a balance of $309.60. Commissioner Gaskill added in the vendue value of the wreck, again less his 5 percent.

To the faraway owners of the latest Outer Banks shipwreck, now relieved of their loss and burden, Commissioner Gaskill after the late February vendue turned over the paltry sum of $333.35.

The schooner *Carroll A. Deering* herself, the ship that had cost a quarter-million to build, stood three weeks pounding on the world's worst shoals, then came apart.

W. O. SAUNDERS
Offices of the Independent
505 East Fearing Street
Elizabeth City, North Carolina
February 26, 1921

You see how Herbert Hoover—who'd not too long ago raised twenty million dollars to feed the starving children of Poland and Yugoslavia and Czechoslovakia and Austria and Germany but *refused* to help out the equally innocent starving children of Russia—finally had his group turn loose of a hundred thousand for Russia? Makes me think a hair better of the new secretary of commerce.

Everybody's so wound up and afraid somebody down the street or up in Washington's going to be helping a Bolshevik and then that Bolshevik's going to turn up right in their hometown, picking their pockets and running off with their women, or their mules, you name it. Some kids, I reckon it was, broke in the school and used the fire hydrant to flood a couple of classrooms—vandalism is what it is and it's worse than sorry, it's just meanness and that's bad enough.

But what does Professor Sheep, whose school it is, say is behind it? Why, *Bolshevism*!

Governor Morrison's come out against the Invisible Knights of the Ku Klux Klan, thank God and the Fourth of July. Now, there really *are* some of them around, somewhere, leaving notes, threats, wanting to run things from behind their veils and under cover of darkness. Well, go on and threaten me some more, Knights. I *still* say, Bolshevism could hardly be worse than invisible government.

NEWS OF THE DAY

The Carolina sound country
February 1921

On Saturday, February 5, the day after Lula Wormell received definite word about the stranded *Deering* and its lost crew, the *News and Observer* of Raleigh, North Carolina, told the world in cold type:

"WILL BE UNABLE TO SAVE SCHOONER OFF HATTERAS." The newspaper said the schooner was valued at $275,000 and would be dynamited after she was stripped for salvage. The great craft was less than two years old.

Nor was the *Deering* the only craft in distress.

In Washington, D.C., some navy men were arrested in a plot to blow up the presidential yacht *Mayflower*. Who would do such a thing? people wondered, and why must there always be trouble with boats and ships?

The four-master *George R. W. Truitt Jr.* caught on Lookout Shoals just a week after the *Deering* hung on the Diamond. Then Warren Harding's yacht *Victoria* sat for two days on a mud reef in Mosquito Lagoon below New Smyrna, Florida, prompting the president-elect, once she was floated free, to extend his Miami-to-the-Keys fishing vacation. In early March the affable adulterer would be sworn in as the nation's twenty-ninth president, and as part of his elevation Harding would kiss George Washington's Bible, his lips right on the verse in Micah that said, "He hath shewed thee, O man, what is good; and what doth the LORD require of thee, but to do justly, and to love mercy, and to walk humbly with thy God?" The Bible-kisser from Blooming Grove, Ohio, would unknowingly let his government lease away the navy's black gold at Teapot Dome, Wyoming, to the oilman Harry Sinclair, and the only mercy of it all for Harding would be the Lord's calling the president home before the scandal really broke, George Washington's good book having long since been returned to Mount Vernon, intact yet having signified nothing.

Elsewhere in America, inventor Thomas Edison turned seventy-four in West Orange, New Jersey. The singer Enrico Caruso lay desperately ill in New York. The anarchists Nicola Sacco and Bartolomeo Vanzetti awaited trial for murder in Massachusetts.

Back in the sound country, in Betsy Town, the riverport on the blackwater Pasquotank that was the closest town of any size to the Outer Banks, the main drive shaft of the cotton mill broke. C. Raymond "Snooks" Evans, star pitcher of the Elizabeth City Twilight League, about to head north to play baseball for the New York Nationals, got a big sendoff banquet, with North Carolina's future governor Blucher Ehringhaus helping lead the salutes.

In New Bern, a man named J. O. Lowder displayed at his shooting gallery a steel pin featuring all 65 words, 254 letters, and 19 punctuations of the Lord's Prayer engraved on its head, the work of three years for a Spokane engraver!

If such things could be, could the missing crew of the *Carroll A. Deering* not also be found?

TWO THE SHIP

LAUNCHING DAY TO JOURNEY'S END,
APRIL 4, 1919–JANUARY 31, 1921

BATH, MAINE: VILLAGE OF SHIPS

In 1841, the shipwrights of Down East Maine launched the *Rappahannock*. At over eleven hundred tons, she was the largest merchant ship ever built in America, and some went so far as to say she was the greatest ship in the history of the world. Six years later, the editor-in-chief of the *New York Evening Post* boarded a steamer in Portland, Maine, bound for the Kennebec River and the upriver capital, Augusta. The boat was the *Huntress*, and the editor was the poet William Cullen Bryant, who took note:

"We passed some small villages where we saw the keels of large unfinished vessels lying high upon the stocks. At Bath, one of the most considerable of these places, but a small village still, were five or six, on which the shipbuilders were busy. These vessels when launched will never be seen again in this place where they were built, but will convey merchandise between the great ports of the world.

"The ship builders of Maine . . . obtain their oak from the Virginia shore, their hard pine from North Carolina."

In this world of shipyards and ropewalks—the largest cordage factory east of Boston was here—Gardiner Deering, son of a ship's carpenter, and William Donnell, son of a master joiner, partnered up in 1866, when Deering was but thirty-three and Donnell twenty-nine. They started in a yard between Marshall and Rose Streets in Bath that till recently had been the workplace of the Hitchcocks, from whom Deering had learned the craft. Their goal was to build small schooners, fishermen, and coasters, and build them to be trim and fast.

In Bath in 1882, two thousand men worked the shipyards, and

twenty-four vessels were on the stocks; fifty of those men, and two ships, were at Deering and Donnell. By the time the two men dissolved their partnership after twenty years, they had built seventy ships.

Then it was Gardiner Deering on his own, storming right on toward the twentieth century, eventually working right alongside the Percy & Small yards, building some of the biggest schooners in the world. It was Gard Deering who came up with the idea of bolting a stout longitudinal shelf for the decking to sit on, thereby revolutionizing deck building with an original design that eliminated knees and strengthened both deck and ship. No one minded this unceremonious man's being a little proud of that.

And no one blamed him for being more than a little chagrined at the accident down at Boston in October 1893, when two Deering-built ships came a-cropper. The outbound four-master *John S. Ames* sailed across the Narrows channel and ploughed into the three-master *Horatio L. Baker*, slicing her starboard to the waterline. The *Ames* crushed her stem in the incident, and the *Baker* lost foremast and main topmast and cracked her mainmast. Gard Deering made it right, though, repairing the *Baker* in his yards at Bath.

On the 20th of April 1905, Deering brought his children formally into the business. He and Frank, Harry, Lydia, and Carroll drew up a one-page letter to themselves, *Articles of Agreement*, in which they agreed thereby to associate themselves "for the purpose of forming a corporation under the laws of the state of Maine for carrying on the business of owning, controlling, managing, building, repairing, buying and selling vessels and vessel property, owning and operating a Marine Railway, or Dry Dock, dealing in real estate, shipbuilding materials and general merchandise, and conducting a Ship brokers and commission business." That just about said it all for this maritime family, and on May 6 they met in the old man's office at 226 Washington Street and became the G. G. Deering Company, Ship Builders and Ship Agents.

During the years of the Great War, the Deerings built one schooner a year for themselves, a five-master in 1916, four-masters in both 1917 and 1918. In 1919—when already ships named *John S. Deering* and *Harry G. Deering* and *Lydia M. Deering* and *Frank M. Deering* and even

The *Carroll A. Deering* during construction, G. G. Deering Company Yards, Washington Street, Bath, Maine.

Gardiner G. Deering were under sail—at the right smart old age of eighty-six, Gard Deering directed the flying of lines and laying of keel and ribbing, the joining and planking and caulking and all the construction and fitting out of his grandest vessel yet, his largest and his last, the five-master he would name for his youngest son, Carroll.

LAUNCHING DAY
G. G. Deering Yards
145–225 Washington Street
Bath, Maine
Friday, April 4, 1919

Late winter's snow lay upon the ways, upon the dark timbers and all about the yard, the spring day that saw the launching of the *Carroll A. Deering*. She flew thirty flags and pennants in her topriggings, including the thirty-three-foot-long burgee, the ship's sailing pennant. Was there a bigger, grander flag anywhere than this spread of white wool bunting, with its deep red borders top and bottom and its dark blue lettering, CARROLL A. DEERING, eight-and-a-half feet top to bottom where it held to her jiggermast and tapering to seven at its swallowtail end?

A tug sat out in the Kennebec, waiting, and one man stood at the oars of a sharp-prowed skiff and moved in for a look at her starboard. Far across the river, pines and cedars on the eastern shore bore mute witness, the front ranks poised above a long ledge of rock that was the gray of unpolished silver. Scores of people stood on the downstream side of the ways, a half a dozen at the little point upstream, two children with flat caps. Another twenty or more crowded the *Deering*'s bow to ride with her down the ways. Her two pendant anchors, over three-and-a-quarter tons each, showed dark against the white of her upper hull. Atop her mainmast was her house flag with its white diamond field, red corners alternating with blue, and the dark blue letter **D** emblazoned upon it, across her stern the lettering

Carroll A Deering
Bath

In a moment the old man Gard Deering would feel her creak beneath him and slowly slide those few all-important feet into the river. Nearly seventy-five years now he had been on the Kennebec, and this great craft was his biggest, her length well over that of the side of a square acre of land. Twenty-one hundred tons of boat.

Yes, he thought, assaying the artwork he and his men had accomplished. And her keel and frame of oak, her ceiling and planking of hard pine. Oregon masts 108 feet tall, topmasts 46 feet. Three decks. The captain's quarters finished out in mahogany and cypress and ash, the midship and forward houses in cypress and Carolina pine. In the forecastle a steam engine called a donkey that under the engineer's hands would power the weighing of anchors and the hoisting of sails.

Six thousand yards of sail!

Since I was twelve, he thought, listening to the ship, its creaking, the

The *Carroll A. Deering*, launching day, April 4, 1919, G. G. Deering Company Yards, Washington Street, Bath, Maine. Length 255.1', beam 44.3', depth 25.3', 2,114 tons.

language of its cordage and spars. Doing this and this alone, since I was twelve. If there is better work, or nobler, what is it? Pray, tell me what it is.

Her other owners were on hand for it all, too, the ones from Bath and a few from beyond—some who held shares in her hailed from Winnegance, Stockton Springs, and Lewiston, Maine, still more from Boston and Quincy, Brookline and Jamaica Plains, Cambridge, Somerville, and Fall River, yet more from New York and Brooklyn, Philadelphia and Baltimore. Most of them were individuals, ponying up $3,750 for a ¹⁄₆₄th share, though a few business names swelled the list, concerns like the Boston Maritime Corporation, the Atlantic Coast Company, the Baltimore Copper Paint Company. G. G. Deering Company, the managing owner, had three shares, and all the Deerings as individuals held pieces of the ship, some as small as ¹⁄₂₅₆th.

Only a few investors held as many as two full shares, and one of these was William Merritt of 21 Day Street, South Portland, Maine. She was part his ship, and he would be her first master.

Yes, they would have a banquet in her honor, sure they would. They would all repair to the King Tavern at Front and Vine just south of the Custom House here in Bath and have a feast: clam stew, olives and radishes, boiled fillet of halibut with hollandaise sauce, sliced cucumbers and duchess potatoes, roast native turkey with cranberry sauce, mashed potatoes and French peas, fruit salad, Parker House rolls, vanilla ice cream, assorted cake, and coffee. But that could wait a little while yet, till after she was lying quiet in the water, at anchor and swinging on her chains for the first time ever.

Workmen below on both sides of the craft now pounded away at the shores and wedges that held the great ship back and set the sliding ways, upon which she sat, free to skid down the greased and tallowed groundways, and the sharp reports of those hammering mauls rang off the side of the dark hull and onto the dark winter water, over the river and into the dark green cedars on the other side. And when the ship's weight could lie no more heavily upon those ways and must move, she began shifting, the tallow smoking fiercely as the hull passed, sliding herself down to the river and toward the ever-beckoning sea beyond.

The mainmast **D** flag flattened — as did all the pennants — to the west in the breeze the ship made as she slid stern first from the Deering yards into the Kennebec River. Gardiner Deering could see that and be proud. Just now Gard Deering could also see his sons Harry and Frank and Carroll and Carroll's wife Annie among the crowd in the *Deering*'s bow, and could hear Annie well as she spoke strongly against the cold April day:

"I christen thee *Carroll A. Deering*!"

With that, she scattered roses and carnations from the bow of the

Launching of the *Carroll A. Deering*, April 4, 1919, Kennebec River at Bath, Maine.

moving ship and the crowd shipboard and the throng ashore roared its cheers and approval with a lustiness that carried all the way to Brunswick, nearly ten miles distant. But no champagne cracked upon her hull, for, as Deering had told the *Bath Enterprise* when they launched the five-masted *Mary F. Barrett* eighteen years earlier:

A

B

Carroll A. Deering,
Kennebec River views:
(A) the *Carroll A. Deering*
with sails bent; (B) davits
and falls at stern of the
Carroll A. Deering, yawl
boat in river around to port;
(C) the *Carroll A. Deering*,
yawl boat on davits

C

"I never christen my vessels. I consider myself lucky if I get them overboard without their sticking."

THE *DEERING* AT WORK

The Atlantic Ocean

1919–1920

Her master's name was William M. Merritt, but seamen and shippers called him "Hungry Bill." He was a hero of the Great War, commended for bravery for his performance under literal fire, losing no men when the German submarine U-117 sank his command, the Deering-built five-masted schooner *Dorothy B. Barrett*, in the waters of the Atlantic off Cape May, New Jersey, in August 1918.

With Captain Merritt at the helm, the *Carroll A. Deering* went into high-dollar trade immediately, first carrying 3,505 tons of coal from Newport News, Virginia, to Rio de Janeiro, Brazil, at $19.50 a ton and paying $800 a ¹⁄₆₄ share on the 20th of May 1919, then returning from Buenos Aires to New York heavy with a 2,912-ton load of Argentine corn at $22 a ton.

Next, on February 11, 1920, or thereabouts, the *Carroll A. Deering* cleared Newport News, shipping 3,261 tons of $20-a-ton coal to the Spanish port of Huelva, this time paying a dividend of $1,240 a ¹⁄₆₄ share. She then hauled 3,460 tons of coal from Baltimore to Guayanilla on Puerto Rico's southern shore, though this coal moved at only $8 a ton, and the *Deering*'s third dividend paid a scant $250 a share. Still, in only a year she'd already earned back for her owners over half their initial investment.

Having sailed for Newport News from Guayanilla and arriving there July 19, the *Carroll A. Deering* then awaited cargo, in August taking on 3,274 tons of $10.90-a-ton coal bound from the Pan Handle Coal Company to Rio. She cleared Hampton Roads August 26, but put in on the 2nd of September, after only a week out, at Lewes, Delaware.

An ill wind blew, and something was wrong.

DOWN EAST VACATION
South Harpswell, Maine
Early September 1920

A young woman swam beyond the breakers, away from the wet rocks in the surf. She was out bathing in the brine with a younger companion, a local girl. The woman wore her long hair pinned up, and her skirted swimming suit was navy blue, as befitted the child of an officer in the nation's merchant marine.

The captain himself—a tall, heavyset man well past sixty, with light wavy hair and a light mustache—stood alone on the rockstrewn beach, pleased to be here with her and her friend rather than far away, as he had spent so much of his life before his recent retirement.

Were they out too far?

Now he paced the beach briskly, as if he were back on the quarter-deck. He was a man never given to staying still, to lighting anywhere long—his arms down at his side, by habit he flexed his hands, from fists to open palms flat down, what he usually did when his men were getting at sixes and sevens with his ship, but now simply out of the nervous excitement of being with his grown daughter. What pleasure it was, though, to be here and see her and witness her health, her strength, her bearing.

His wife stayed back at the cottage, not far from the beach but far enough. She would not swim, she would not watch, nor would she even venture seaward at all during their respite at South Harpswell, their fourth season here. She much preferred the family's life back in the city of Portland, in their Lawn Avenue home miles from the sea. There, though she still feared the ocean that she and her family and her whole city lived upon (as did all along the involuted and raggedy-rocked coast of Maine), she need never look upon it, and she did not.

The family was on vacation the third summer following the armistice that ended The Great War, and it was hot now even in Maine, even here on the coast of Casco Bay. The woman swimming was Lula Wormell, and her father, a well-known, lifelong veteran of the coast-wise and West Indies schooner trade, was Captain Willis B. Wormell.

WORD FROM DELAWARE

The Hotel Rodney
Delaware Breakwater, Lewes, Delaware
September 6, 1920

From the day of her launching forward, "Hungry Bill" Merritt had been master of the *Carroll A. Deering*, the only one she had known, but just now the fifty-four-year-old captain found himself ashore and laid low, cramped and afflicted in a hotel room here in Lewes, the little bayport west of Cape Henlopen at the mouth of Delaware Bay.

Captain Willis B. Wormell of Portland, Maine

Anchored inside the cape since September 2, the *Deering* was filled with coal, for like her cousins, the other four- and five- and six-masted giant schooners, the *Deering* was a collier, built to carry Pennsylvania coal that the railroads brought to Philadelphia, or West Virginia coal railed down to Norfolk and Newport News, on from those coalports coastwise up and into New England at Boston or Portland, where the huge gantry cranes and grab buckets of the Maine Central Railroad would unload them at the water's edge into the waiting strings of hoppercars on the wharf, and even farther Down East, even to Bath.

The Great War to make the world safe for democracy had certainly transformed the work of America's coastwise colliers, turning them into hemispheric shippers, because the nations of Latin America during wartime could no longer import European coal. The Latin nations turned to the north and the great American schooners became the conduits.

The *Carroll A. Deering* was outward bound for Rio de Janeiro, but her captain lay too ill, and after five days trying and failing to shake it knew he was not the man who would see the schooner's voyage through.

Back in Norfolk, Merritt had told the ship's supplier, Mr. Pendleton at William H. Swan Sons on Monticello Avenue, that he was feeling unwell, and, further, that he did not like his crew and did not want to sail with them. His previous crew—a Portuguese bos'n, Norwegian cook, and six able-bodieds, most of them from Cape Verde—he had paid off in July, and they refused to sign on for the current trip, none wanting to agree to articles specifying that they would "load or discharge cargo or ballast, or both, if required by master." Only the mate—his son—and the engineer—donkeyman Herbert Bates—stayed on, and then he'd had a devil of a time finding the rest of his crew for the sail to Rio. The Scandinavian Julius Nelson, agent of the Eastern and Gulf Sailors Association and a man thought by many around Hampton Roads shipping circles to be a radical and a disturber, found Merritt his Finnish bos'n, his six Danish sailors.

Now, in Lewes, Captain Merritt directed his son, First Mate S. E. Merritt, to wire Gardiner Deering back in Bath, Maine, and request a relief captain, suggesting for the job his Portland neighbor, the renowned schoonerman Willis B. Wormell.

LULA WORMELL

South Harpswell, Maine
September 1920

If there were ever a time when people called me something other than the captain's daughter, I cannot remember it. Captain Wormell's girl. And I was, I always knew, his heart's delight.

—Oh, you're the captain's daughter—Lord, he must be proud of *you*!

—You got a real sweet little girl there, Willis.

—Not a lot of girls as lucky as you are, Lula, fine a daddy as you have. I bet you really enjoy going around everywhere with him.

Yes, everywhere around Portland, where we lived, and Bath, certainly. But not really *everywhere* with him, though I would have shipped out with him in a trice, and gladly, too, as much as I loved the sea. Just like him. That's where I'd have been, were I a boy, had I been born, as Queen Elizabeth once said, crested and not cloven. But fate's fate, and it was Father's lot and his alone to leave us, Mother and me, two or three times a year, hauling coal around the East, bringing lumber back from the South. When there was a breeze to be had, he found it, ran before it, saved money, *made* money for the ship-owners and how they loved *that*—and him, too, for it.

Even when the *Alice M. Lawrence*, that big six-master, went aground with Father at the helm, no one faulted him.

How could they? That was in a gale, in December of '14, and the winds blew them onto the Tuckernuck Island shoals in Nantucket Sound.

And not just onto the shoals, either, but upon another wreck there, upon the very bones of the *Van Gilder*, a ship that had lost itself and its load of stone in that same rough place. Did you think for a moment the *Lawrence* could take that? Of course not—it broke her very back! Father and his crew stayed with her for a week and a half—he even entertained someone for *breakfast* out there on the wreck!—salvaging her rigging, her block-and-tackle, any gear they could take off her before giving her over to the sea.

And he was home for Christmas.

Well, that was six years ago, and after that I can't tell you how glad Mother was when Father told us he was leaving the sea, what joy she took in those words! Oh, he's made a few trips, short ones, nothing like being gone weeks and months at a time, just favors to the owners now and again. Mother even allowed as how that was a good thing, that a man just couldn't give up *all* he'd known and done and followed for his whole life, and that, besides, we wouldn't want to get spoiled, having him around all the livelong day.

So it's all seemed to be working out.

At least, till this telegram showed up from the Deerings. Would he consider one more run for them?

One more long run?

CHECKING OUT

South Harpswell, Maine
September 7, 1920

A knock came at the door of the Stover family this morning, and Miriam—Lula Wormell's young swimming and rowboating companion—answered and let Captain Wormell into the front hall. She then led him into the sitting room, where her father was reading the *Portland Evening Express* from the day before.

"Stover," said Captain Wormell, pulling the set of skeleton keys to their cottage from his coat pocket in an anxious motion and handing them to the other man. "I'm taking Mrs. Wormell and Lula back to Portland a bit early. I've just received a message from the owners of the *Carroll A. Deering* to take command of her at Lewes, Delaware, and proceed to Rio—Captain Merritt is ill and can't continue."

"Well, sure," said Stover. "I can understand that. Man who knows how's got to work. Rockin' chair ain't got you yet, Cap."

"Don't reckon."

"No, you go on. No charge this week, you're only one day into it. Where you say you're taking this . . ."

"Schooner, 5-master."

"Schooner."

Captain Wormell and kin aboard the schooner *Alice M. Lawrence*: (left to right) Arthur Gillard, Captain Wormell, Castella Wormell Gillard, Eva Gillard Stearns, Flora Gillard.

"Brazil," said Captain Wormell. "Rio de Janeiro, Brazil."

"Long way, there, yeah. And back."

Overhearing all this, Miriam rushed over to the Wormells' cottage, found Lula, and embraced her tearfully. "Now, now," Lula comforted her friend. "You come to see me in Portland this winter sometime and spend the night at Lawn Avenue. You'll like it, I know you will."

And that was all. The Wormells, father and daughter anyhow, were disappointed to leave the small beach community, the Stovers likewise sorry to see them go. But Willis Wormell, despite his being retired and sixty-six years old, had stayed on call as an interim captain and was now bound as if pulled by the ebb tide herself down to the sea yet again.

The deck of Captain Wormell's command, the six-masted schooner *Alice M. Lawrence*, in port at Brooklyn, N.Y.

SOUTH TO DELAWARE
The Eastern Seaboard
September 7, 1920

A great, coal-laden schooner swung heavily on her chains in Delaware Bay, costing her owners and awaiting her new master. The Wormells caught the southbound train of the Maine Central in Brunswick, a few miles north of Harpswell, and Captain Wormell debarked with his wife and daughter at Woodfords Station, Portland, and went with them to Lawn Avenue just long enough to collect his grip, his canvas bag, and his seachest from home. He got back to the Portland station just in time to make the next Boston and Maine train, changed in Boston—where he quickly collected a new first mate, Charles McLellan, for the *Deering*—to the New York, New Haven, and Hartford line, and rode the rods on into Manhattan's nearly new Grand Central Station.

What a castle of transport, he marveled, as he strode the great marble-floored hall, his steps joining the shunt and shuffle of hundreds of other travelers. Above them all, in the vaulted blue ceiling the zodiacal constellations blinked and twinkled away. Outside, the midtown streets of New York City were mobbed with soldiers in uniform, some still actively in service and some just on the bum, with European refugees from the Great War abroad, with black men and women and children everywhere, refugees from the Southland, where the boll weevil's thirty years of eating its way across the region had finally crashed cotton and driven them off the farms.

In the noise and haste and din of Pershing Square, Captain Wormell flagged a hack and got his and his mate's gear stowed and ordered the driver west, past the drummers' hotels and former brass-railed bars of Forty-second Street, down Seventh Avenue to the Romanesque colonnades and pavilions of Pennsylvania Station. He passed through the city only a week too soon to be there when radicals tried to blow up Wall Street with a TNT bomb that killed thirty and wounded hundreds—a coalfield operator on the scene said it was without a doubt the doing of Bolsheviks. By September 16, when a shrapnel bomb blew apart the driverless wagon and eviscerated the horse that had drawn it up before J. P. Morgan's imperial offices, Captain Wormell would be far out at sea, ferrying his load of coal south to the Brazilians, and would miss the horrific occasion and only hear of it much later.

This evening he boarded the train for Trenton, Philadelphia, and Wilmington, where he changed to the last train of the night going on down through Delaware, through little flatland farmtowns with names like Bear and Blackbird, Woodside and Lincoln and Georgetown, where the truck farms and market gardens grew.

In waterside Lewes the Hotel Rodney stood big, many-gabled, and tall—five stories in all, a porch wrapping around much of its second

The Hotel Rodney, Lewes, Del.

floor. The Rodney was a first-class hostelry with a restaurant, with pool tables as well in the now-quiet ground-floor bar. Tourists stayed there, Coast Guardsmen and navymen too, and men who worked at the fish house would form up there and walk on to work. "Meet you at the Rodney house" was a saying around Lewes, and the old hotel that dated to the mid-1880s afforded a magnificent overlook of the beach, the breakwater and harbor, and the vast Delaware Bay beyond.

By the time Captain Wormell and First Mate McLellan signed the register at the Rodney they were worn out, and the night was half gone. On the morning of the 8th of September, they would sign articles as master and mate with the deputy collector of the Port of Lewes. Willis

Wormell had answered the Deering family's call without hesitation and could have journeyed no more quickly than he had to become the new and final master of the *Carroll A. Deering*.

Captains Merritt and Wormell of Maine would meet at the Rodney. If theirs was but a brief moment, it was still long enough to exchange greetings and, by transferring the mastery of the schooner *Deering*, to exchange their very fates.

LETTER FROM RIO

Aboard the Carroll A. Deering
At the wharf, Rio de Janeiro, Brazil
November 21, 1921

Dear Brother Cecil—

My wife sent me Clare's letter and I am quite surprised to hear that you are so poorly. I intended to write to you before I left home but everything seemed to be in a flurry so I did not get a chance to write you but I do hope by the time you receive this you will be feeling better. Trust in the Lord and pray earnestly for help and He will hear your prayers and answer them. Cecil, I believe there is no better help can be had than what we get from our Master. Oh be faithful and watch and pray with thanksgiving. I would not give up the hope I have in my Master for worlds like this. I would like very much to see you all but be good. You know the Bible says look at the generations of old, and see; did ever any trust in the Lord and was confounded? Or did any abide in His fear, and was forsaken? Or whom did He ever despise, that called upon Him? Ecclesiastes ii 10.

I sometimes feel the thread of life is slender,
And soon with me the labour will be wrought;
Then grows my heart to other hearts more tender
The time is short.

Thanks be unto God for His unspeakable gift—2 Corinthians ix.15.

Now my dear Brother let us hope and pray and pray good and strong for His goodness to the children of men. I will say good day for this time and hope to see you all some time. By. By. Willis

TWO CAPTAINS ABOARD SHIP

Aboard the Governor Brooks
Rio de Janeiro, Brazil
Sunday, November 28, 1920

In Rio de Janeiro the wharves did not have the luxurious commercial appointments of the coal docks back in the States—no gantry cranes could help unload the colliers from on high. Here they had to warp right alongside the bulkheads and use their own hoisting engines to pull the coal forth from their holds, and dark men stripped to the waist shoveled it the livelong day into wagons, carts, wheelbarrows.

During this slow and slovenly process the *Carroll A. Deering* had a familiar neighbor at the wharf. Namesake of Wyoming's rancher-governor Bryant Brooks, launched in October '07 by the next Bath ship-builder up the Kennebec River from Gard Deering—Percy & Small—and christened by the governor's daughter Abby with a toss over the bow of roses and pinks, the five-masted *Governor Brooks* had lain up for repairs in Rio since July 1920. Almost as soon as she had pulled into port, her seams opened by a gale, another ship struck her.

George A. Goodwin, the *Brooks*'s captain, hailed from Lubec, Maine, where Captain Wormell was born, and the two men were longtime friends—each for a time had captained the same four-masted schooner, the *Alicia B. Crosby.* Sunday afternoon they spent out and about touring Rio by shank's mare and donkey-drawn streetcar. Back at the wharves, aboard the *Governor Brooks* and in the captain's cabin, Wormell now leveled with his peer:

"I have a worthless mate," he said. "Second mate not much better. But should anything out of the ordinary occur, I have a good engineer from Islesboro, Maine, and he'll stick by me."

"Who's that?" asked Goodwin.

"You know him yourself. His name is Herbert Bates."

"Oh, yes. Good man, Bates."

"Yes. So at least there's that, thank God."

And they spoke a few moments of Bates, who would soon join them for dinner, with a sad reverence toward him, for his having had two brothers and a sister-in-law all lost at sea with a schooner sailing from Tallahassee twenty years earlier, another ship that never made port.

The schooner *Carroll A. Deering* cleared Rio de Janeiro on Thursday, December 2, 1920, bound for Hampton Roads, Virginia, by way of Bridgetown, Barbados. The schooner *Governor Brooks* would not leave Rio for over two months yet, and her fortunes would worsen almost immediately with more bad weather as she stood for Montevideo, Uruguay. Captain Goodwin and his crew would abandon their leaking ship off Cape Castillo, and a British steamer would come upon the deserted schooner shortly thereafter and torch the derelict. Goodwin's men would reach land in safety, but what was left of the *Governor Brooks* in the south Atlantic—witnessed for the last time a week after she burned, her deck awash, only four of her five poles now to the sky—would pass on into oblivion.

THE ENGINEER WRITES HOME

Aboard the Carroll A. Deering
At the wharf, Rio de Janeiro, Brazil
November 30, 1920

Dear Mother. Just a few lines this morning to say Hello. Expect to finish discharging today and will Probaly go to sea Dec. 2d. We are going to Barbados for Orders. will Probaly go to Norfolk from there. Don't know yet. I was on board the Schr *Governor Brooks* Sunday and had Dinner She is in here in distress been here six months I sprained my ankle there Sunday and I am all most a Cripple since. Its not very painful only swollen very badly. Guess I will be alright in a few days I haven't much work to do for a few days so will not have to stand up very much. I dread the Cold weather but will be in it in about six weeks I expect I haven't seen any American newspapers since being here. Therefore I don't know any news. That's all for now. You Can see in the Paper where the schr is going from barbados if to Hampton Roads Va you can write me in care of schr *Carroll A. Deering* c/o Clark Tow Boat Company Norfolk Va hope These few lines will find you making out alright—Love from Herb

From the December heat of the Tropic of Capricorn the *Deering* departed on Thursday, December 2, and sailed up the Brazilian coast and around the great headland of the Ponta do Calcanhar, past Fortaleza and the mouth of the majestic, deltic Amazon and all its equatorial broil. When she was southbound for Rio, the *Carroll A. Deering* slogged heavily through the seas, her cargo of thousands of tons of coal holding her down low in the water and her decks most always wet, but now on the return to the north she rode high and bright on the seas, her long hull a great sail in and of itself, and fresh breezes hitting her abeam could send her almost skittering to leeward across the ocean's surface like a cork.

Past Devil's Island she plied, at last passing Captain Wormell's old familiar haunts of Trinidad and the straits that led to Port of Spain—the Dragon's Mouths—thence round Needham's Point on southwest Barbados and on into Carlisle Bay.

Once the schooner took in sail and slowed and stilled and the *Carroll A. Deering* dropped her hooks in Bridgetown harbor, First Mate McLellan picked a fight with Captain Wormell. When the mate let fly with the threat, "I'll kill you before it's over, old man," Wormell ordered him off the ship at once—whereupon the crew, led by McLellan, hit the waterfront shebangs and pulled an uproarious five-day drunk. McLellan slammed about town, eventually in sufficient disorder and disarray to win himself a stay in the Bridgetown brig, and after the instigator's arrest the Scandinavians got deeper into the rum and only much later returned to the schooner mad, ill, and dark of mood.

WHAT CAPTAIN NORTON HEARD
Bridgetown, Barbados
Early January 1921

When they spoke, Captain Wormell told Captain Hugh L. Norton, master of the schooner *Augusta W. Snow*, that he was having serious trouble with his mate, Charles McLellan.

"He's been habitually drunk while ashore," said Captain Wormell, "and he's utterly unable to handle the crew properly. Here in Bridgetown he's been ashore drunk most of the time. He treats the men brutally, totally uncalled for."

Captain Norton thought Wormell appeared to be in excellent health—though others in the Barbadian ship chandlers' and agents' offices of Da Costa and Company, notably Mr. Foster the solicitor and Mr. Lewis the boarding officer, visited with Captain Wormell when he came in for orders and took him to be a sick man.

"Where's the *Deering* bound from Barbados?" asked Captain Norton.

"Hampton Roads," Captain Wormell said.

"And from there?"

"I don't know. I'll not go any farther with her once I've brought her to Virginia. I'll be going on home to Maine."

Later at Da Costa's Captain Norton happened to see McLellan, the *Deering*'s mate, whom he judged partially sober.

"Having trouble with my crew," McLellan volunteered.

"Is that a fact?" said Captain Norton.

"Considerable trouble, on account of they refuse to work. And times I've wanted to punish them, Captain Wormell steps in, interfering, interceding in their behalf—so I've got no authority, and can't do anything with them. On top of that, I've had to do all the navigating, working out all the sights."

"You?"

"Captain Wormell's eyesight's so bad he has to wear double glasses. He can't take any sights."

"Well."

"Truth is, I need a new ship, sir," McLellan said.

"You *what*?"

"I wish you'd sign me on as mate."

Captain Norton had to wonder what sort of creature he was regarding. McLellan did not look good to him, did not impress him as a man he could depend on. Yet he spoke good English and said he was a naturalized American with years of experience sailing the Atlantic Coast.

Still, Wormell's words were those of a fellow captain, and they rang true.

"No, Mr. McLellan."

"But, Captain—"

"No, sir, and that'll be the last of it."

In the Continental Café in Barbados, First Mate Sippi of the *Snow*, as well as Captain Norton and the captain of the *Alice M. Colburn*, heard McLellan raise his voice in boastful threat against Captain Wormell, claiming,

"Well, then, I'll get the captain before we get to Norfolk. I will."

TWO CAPTAINS ALONG THE SHORE
Near Bridgetown, Barbados
Early January 1921

Again Captain Wormell sought out a friend and fellow ship's captain—G. W. Bunker of Calais, Maine—and together they walked the Barbadian beach, out near the towers and the windmill of the British prison at Saint Ann's Garrison, Wormell nearly exhausted now by the extra work that fell to him and by the strain of bearing up against the unruliness of the schooner's crew, the worst—he said again and again in virtual disbelief—in his entire career.

"Would they turn on you?" Captain Bunker asked.

Wormell paused, but not out of surprise. He had given that question no small amount of thought already, as indeed every captain since the Phoenicians had so wondered. Every master would have his mettle tested by the sea and by the men who said first with their signatures and then by their work and obedience that they trusted him to lead them through and over and across it.

"Not all of them, I don't think," Wormell said at last.

"Well, that's good, as far as it goes," Bunker said.

"What do you mean?"

"I mean it doesn't take all of them, you know that. Doesn't even take the main bunch, just a few of them, armed."

"Yes."

Bunker stopped, relit his pipe. The waves rolling in before them were light and reassuring, and the cumulus clouds at the back of the huge blue sky were highpiled like southern cotton in wagons waiting at a gin. It was always like this: a rude peace in port, the able-bodieds gone in one direction to get away from the old man, the old men (so called, no matter what their age, by their men and so consigned prematurely to be historic figures and as such to be eminently testable and prodded in order for their nominal lessers to learn were they like men of history of two dimensions and cardboard only? were they names only, these captains? when the sailors pushed them, would the captains push back?) finding each other to review, to compare and prepare, with one passage just made and its former uncertainty become the artifact of a done deed and with the next and yet unmade passage in the offing as inscrutable as the sea beyond the horizon, as if it were the dark side of the moon that lay east of the Sea of Crises, west of the Ocean of Storms.

Two men walking slowly along the shore at Bridgetown in January could hardly be faulted for slowing their pace, for lingering there, for hanging on to their time, knowing as they must how very far away this perpetual summerland of the Windwards was from the massive tides and fierce winter winds of Down East Maine or even from the treacherous nor'easters that so often pounded Carolina's closer coast. After a spell Captain Bunker said:

"I am thinking of the *Senator Schroeder*."

"Ah, yes," said Wormell.

"You know of her, then?"

"A little—heard her name a lot last summer."

"And well you might've."

"German, wasn't she?" said Captain Wormell.

"Yes, a fishing schooner from one of the northern ports. Crew of fourteen and only one was a mutineer. You see what I mean."

"Just the one? I took it there were more."

"Oh, there were two stowaways, and he enlisted them. Bound for Iceland, wound up in Russia," said Captain Bunker. "Bad business."

"Is that what you call it?"

"Or bad men. Where're yours from, anyhow?"

"My sorry mate's a sot I picked up in Boston," said Captain Wormell. "My cook's from Boston, too. Engineer's a Down Easter, a good man and one I've known, and six seamen, all Danes."

"The bos'n?"

"Frederickson—he's from Finland."

"Jesus, a Finn."

"All right, all right."

There was hardly a sailor anywhere in the world who was not prone to superstition. But these were modern times, and Willis Wormell was a God-fearing man, not given to antique notions about a seaman's nationality being enough to cause shipboard vexation—Jonahs, seamen called badluck men—and put a man's command on the bottom.

"The thing is, Bunker, to make them do it they'd have to want something."

"My God, man—they'd want the *ship*, isn't that enough?"

"No, I don't believe so. They'd have to want to get something more out of it. Besides, we've no cargo, nothing for them to start with— we're light from Rio. What would they do with an empty vessel?"

"Just watch them, Willis."

"You know I will."

"And watch them all. If you're even worrying about one, you watch them all as if each is the one you've reason to fear. And maybe you *are* sailing light, but this place is a rumbucket and maybe it's in somebody's plan you won't *be* so light from Bridgetown."

The two captains turned and made their way back down the beach toward town, where the *Deering*'s mate lay in irons and the ship's crew lay out in a grogshop. As the men came closer to Bridgetown again, Captain Wormell could see yonder, in a small seaside cemetery upon higher ground, several figures hiding themselves from the sun in thatch lean-tos set against the crypts. Were they living there? he wondered. Or were they waiting furtively for the sea, by prearranged design or by chance, to bring them something? He suddenly judged himself too suspicious and gave no voice to his thoughts. Enough—no further word of smuggling or conspiracy. For any more of such a drift, the Barbadian afternoon was too fair.

On Sunday, the 9th of January, Captain Wormell forgave First Mate McLellan, bailed him out of the Bridgetown jail, and got him back on ship in less than the best shape. He ordered his obstreperous crew to weigh anchor, and the *Carroll A. Deering* cleared Barbados for Hampton Roads, Virginia, and in so doing bade farewell to the last port she would ever make.

WHAT CAPTAIN NORTON SAW

Aboard the Augusta W. Snow
Latitude 26°56'N
Longitude 76°31'W
Off Abaco, Bahamas
January 16, 1921

Captain Hugh Norton of the *Snow*, who had heard such conflicting stories of the *Deering*'s shipboard life back in Barbados from Captain Wormell and First Mate McLellan, and then in a café there had witnessed McLellan's death threat against Wormell, saw some queer doings at sea about a week after the *Snow* cleared Bridgetown.

This Sunday, at 9:30 in the morning, Captain Norton spied a five-masted schooner five miles to leeward. The five-master had up but a single mainsail, though Norton knew the weather at the time would have allowed for more sail.

She's out of control, he thought, as he watched her make a zigzag, switchback course and then swing around in a southerly way, the opposite direction the *Deering* should and would be sailing—if indeed she *were* the *Deering*. Whatever ship it was, and he never got any closer to her than those five miles and could never say for certain, Captain Norton reckoned the vessel's performance rather strange, as he stood at the rail of the *Snow*, thinking,

Trouble on board.

THE FRYING-PAN-TO-LOOKOUT STORM

The North Carolina capes

Sunday, January 23–Friday, January 28, 1921

What a difference for the *Deering* a fortnight would make.

At 4 P.M. on January 18, she was opposite Cape Canaveral off the Florida coast, and by the 20th she had sailed to a point off Beaufort, South Carolina.

Then, two weeks after sailing away from the balminess of Barbados and making the long, lazy S-curve around the Windwards, the Leewards, the Bahamas, and standing for the Carolinas, on Sunday, January 23, the *Carroll A. Deering* passed the Frying Pan light vessel between 4 and 5 P.M., hauling eastward to a course of northeast by east. The breeze was gentle out of the west and southwest, the sky a clear blue, the seas smooth, and the temperature a moderate sixty degrees when the *Deering* cleared Frying Pan Shoals and Cape Fear, North Carolina.

Over the next week, though, very heavy weather came after the schooner, the lightships, and all the coastal waters of Carolina.

By Wednesday, January 26, the seas at the Frying Pan light vessel were rough, and a northeast wind, nearly a gale, was blowing drizzling mists and rains over her decks.

Light Vessel 80, lying off Lookout Shoals, was steel hulled and no small steamship—with a length overall of 129', two steel masts and wooden spencers, her stack amidships, and a small wheelhouse forward. To her, Wednesday the 26th brought mists, hail, snow, fog, and gale winds out of the northeast, freshening on through the day and night.

On Thursday, January 27, the Lookout Shoals light vessel reported gale winds all night and all day, up to fifty miles an hour out of the northeast by noon, sixty by 8 o'clock that evening, and blowing a hurricane, seventy-five miles an hour, by 10 P.M. that night. Everything aboard her was battened down, but, with the seas breaking steadily over the lightship, water forced its way in under the skylight, into the cabin, drenching the crew's bedding.

On Friday, January 28, the winds eased their attack on *Light Vessel 80*, steadily decreasing to fifty by 6 A.M., to forty-five by noon, to thirty-five by midnight.

The storm seemed to have spent itself; the worst seemed to have passed.

HAILING
Light Vessel 80
Off Cape Lookout, North Carolina
Latitude 34°18'27"N
Longitude 76°24'18"W
Saturday, January 29, 1921
4:30 P.M.

The northeast wind that had blown such a gale, such a heavy roaring nor'easter for days now, slackened Saturday all day long. The sailors on *Light Vessel 80* started and stopped the bells and fog whistles three times, as the wind came down from thirty-five miles an hour in the night to twenty-five at dawn, to ten and foggy at noon. By later in the afternoon, a calm had come over the cape and its shoals, with the sea smooth and breezes blowing lightly now out of the south-southwest. At 4 P.M. the temperature was fifty-four degrees.

Presently a five-masted schooner drew nigh from the south, all sails set. She was a powerful sight, and James Steel, the Lookout lightship's engineer, stepped to the rail and photographed her as she approached, coming in close. Someone would later recall that the sailor who hailed them was a red-headed man, and that his accent was foreign. He used a megaphone, and cried out:

"We've lost both anchors and chains in the gale off Frying Pan Shoals—forward word to our owners!"

As the *Carroll A. Deering* sailed past at about four knots, Thomas Jacobson, the lightship's master, noted that the schooner's crew were scattered in an undisciplined fashion about the deck, particularly about the quarterdeck—the captain's province, his and his alone, sacrosanct.

The *Carroll A. Deering* passing and hailing *Lookout Shoals Light Vessel 80*.
View from the lightship, Saturday, January 29, 1921, 4:30 P.M.

The man who hailed the lightship to Jacobson did not look or act or speak like either the master or an officer—his speech was broken, and Jacobson took him for a Scandinavian.

Where, then, is the captain? Jacobson wondered.

He thought the *Deering* was making excellent time, with all sails set and the jib topsail slacked down (at head hanging in clew), and that she looked very trim and neat in passing.

The wireless aboard the lightship was not working, though, and so, for good or ill, no word could go forth. Away to the north the schooner sailed, dropping down beyond the horizon, while simultaneously there appeared a southbound steamer, carrying antenna for wireless. Captain Jacobson of the lightship would hail the steamer, now, and pass the schooner's word on through her. He quickly hoisted flags with the International Code Signal Letters RQK:

"Have important message."

The steamer never even slowed down.

The lightship master then blew four blasts on his Number 12 steam whistle, a powerful, fog-warning shriek with a range of five miles. At this alarm, widely honored on the high seas, the steamer changed her course and now went sailing eastward, full speed ahead, as crewmen unfurled a canvas to cover the ship's nameplate on her stern.

"The passing steamer, being too far away to read her name and signals to her being ignored, is unknown to me," Thomas Jacobson would later write in a June 18, 1921, letter to the superintendent of lighthouses in Baltimore. "The appearance of the vessel showed a black hull of 3,000 or 3,500 tons capacity, two masts, one black painted stack, placed amidship with house and bridge." A British tramp, he thought she was.

Jacobson was sufficiently unnerved at the time to have remarked in his deck log that the sailing ship was a "4 mast schooner" and to have recorded her passing as having occurred late in the afternoon of Friday the 28th of January, rather than on Saturday the 29th, when it actually happened. His reason for so doing, he would also report several months hence to the superintendent of lighthouses, was "some unaccountable error." There had been hurricane-force winds buffeting the Carolina coast earlier in the week, and, by their own deck-log notations, almost all day that Saturday Jacobson and his men had found themselves in clouds, in haze, in a fog.

In a fog.

Lookout Shoals Light Vessel 80, early twentieth century. Length 129', beam 28'6",
draft 12'6", 668 tons.

"SHE APPEARED TO BE
STEERING FOR CAPE HATTERAS"

Atlantic shipping lanes
Off North Carolina
Sunday, January 30, 1921
3:30 P.M.–8:32 P.M.

Bound from Sagua la Grande on the north coast of Cuba for its
home port of Baltimore on the last Sunday in January was the steamship *Lake Elon*.

At about 3:30 in the afternoon, Captain Henry Johnson sighted a
five-masted schooner two points off the *Elon*'s starboard bow. Much
later, from Havana on the 27th of June, the master and his mate would

wire Secretary Herbert Hoover's Department of Commerce in Washington, recalling:

> The wind was S.W. moderate and she had all sails set and steering about NNW making about seven miles. We passed her about 5:45 P.M. about one-half mile off on our port side we were then about twenty-five miles S.W. true from the Diamond Shoal Light Vessel, from the description of the *Deering*, we think that this schooner was her but we could not read her name, there was nothing irregular to be seen on board this vessel but she was steering a peculiar course.
>
> She appeared to be steering for Cape Hatteras.
>
> We sighted Diamond Shoal Light Vessel about 7 P.M. and passed it 8:32 P.M.
>
> The lookout on the schooner should have sighted Cape Hatteras Light, also the Light ship at Diamond Shoal a little later than we did but in plenty time to avoid going on shore as the weather was clear and cloudy with a good visibility. There were a couple of more ships in the vicinity steering a course parallel with us which should have convinced the Captain of the schooner that he was steering a wrong course.
>
> Hoping that this may be of some value we are
> Very truly yours,
> Henry Johnson
> Master, SS *Lake Elon*
> E. V. Ferrandini, Chief Officer

At 8 P.M. Sunday evening, January 30, another ship sailed past Cape Hatteras, reporting the wind at that time to be a fresh breeze from out of the west, the weather clear. Some would say she sailed that day and night in company with the *Carroll A. Deering*, but it was not so, according to Captain W. K. Andersen. He would beat against a north wind the next day, with a daylight haze lingering on and staying with him all the way to Cape Henry, Virginia, where he anchored at 10 P.M.

Of the *Deering's* men, the master of this schooner would later record a straightforward-enough comment, yet one with an odd resonance — for Captain Andersen himself sailed in command of uncertainty constant, his ship a namesake for the first white child born in America, the babe born and borne away without a trace among Walter Raleigh's Roanoke Island colony in 1587, her name coequal with the vanished, the disappeared, and the lost.

"What could have happened to the *Deering*'s Capt. and Crew if they were aboard," wrote the master of the *Virginia Dare*, "is a mystery to me."

THREE
THE SEARCH
AND BEYOND

MARCH–AUGUST 1921,

SEPTEMBER 1921–JUNE 1948

W. O. SAUNDERS

Offices of the Independent
505 East Fearing Street
Elizabeth City, North Carolina
March 11, 1921

Oh, did I notice what was at play in this case here? You bet your life I did!

Just give this Perquimans County boy a yarn, especially a yarn of the sea, and I'm off and running. But like everybody around here knows, I'm straight up and I *do* write em the way I see em, and the elements were plain as day: "A stout New England shipmaster weathered to all the gales that blow trod her quarter deck. . . . Under the drive of her sail the ship was buried beyond the power of tugs to pull her out."

Simple enough, wouldn't you say? Sure, sure. If it's that simple, though, let's just look at it again: that captain knew Diamond Shoals were there, and yet he struck his ship and ran her hard aground and he had all his canvas out. Now, how came an old salt to do that? And having done that, how came he then to order his men to abandon ship, to take to the ship's boats in the dead of night and go down in the dark into the hideous breakers and the rough, rough surf without being able to see at all what was going on?

W. O. Saunders, editor of the *Independent*, Elizabeth City, N.C.

You tell me—does any of that sound like the work of a man who knew the oceans of the world?

I can see what's simple, but I have to wonder awhile about what's not. All I say's that beyond what we know and *can* see, all manner of things move about in the mists, and who knows but it'll be a spell before this case comes clear. Might take some time, all right—but what we've got here on Main Street, Elizabeth City, way down yonder on the Pasquotank, where the bullfrogs jump from bank to bank, is just that—*time*. And if it turns out some agency beyond human is at play here with the *Carroll Deering*, well, I just want everybody to remember that I nicknamed her, all right — and that you saw it first here in the *Independent*:

"Ghost Ship of Diamond Shoals."

THE CUTTER *SEMINOLE*
Off Hatteras Island, North Carolina
March 15–16, 1921

Searching off the great shoals for the broken-up *Carroll A. Deering* six weeks after she foundered, the *Seminole* came across her stern section late in the day on the Ides of March. At 5:10 P.M., the *Seminole* made the position of the *Deering's* floating wreckage to be latitude 35°16'N and longitude 75°17'W — a bit up the Carolina coast above Cape Hatteras and a very good ways out to sea.

The *Seminole* found quite a sizable piece of the wreck, about seventy-five feet by thirty, comprising the port side, counter, poop deck, after house, and house deck, her name showing on the port bulwarks. Her men made a line fast and tried to tow the wreck in to Hatteras Cove, but the *Seminole* and her burden steamed into a strong outbound current and were swept eastward. After trying all night to counter this force, and failing, the *Seminole's* commander now figured that his craft and tow had lost nearly eleven miles drifting northeast during the night.

At a quarter past eight the morning of March 16, the *Seminole* cast off the hawser and discontinued the towing. She then spent the morning placing and setting off five gun-cotton mines and reported "the wreckage being completely broken up and no longer a menace to navigation at 11:45 A.M., in Latitude 35 degrees, 22 minutes North, Longitude 75 degrees, 07 minutes West."

Already, after the ship's late February breakup on outer Diamond Shoals, the bow section had floated south toward Ocracoke, and that was that.

Or was it?

What else might fetch up before the winter and equinoctial storms had had their way with this wild coast?

What else indeed?

CHRISTOPHER COLUMBUS GRAY

Buxton Beach
Cape Hatteras, North Carolina
March 16, 1921

A man likes to walk the beach looking for drift, a man does, especially an old navy man like me. I say old—hell, I'm just thirty-five, but I've already done three tours in the navy—Atlantic, Pacific, European waters too—and that adds up on a man. Coal passer, fireman second class *and* first class on the USS *Virginia*, and then I was oiler on the USS *Connecticut*—and on the USS *Indiana* they made me water tender and *chief* water tender, honorably discharged from each tour, each ship.

Oh, I've got the wife and boy here at the house, but I've still got plenty of knocking about left in me, sure I do. Anybody thinks he can count me out just yet, well, he's got another think coming, is what I say. And you want to know what's going on around here, I'm your man. Reckon I'm out on this beach more than anybody—fishing, checking the tide line, seeing what old Neptune's flung up and left me of a morning. Why, half the stuff I've got in my house up there's come off this beach, planks and net-floats and, hell, even my little three-legged stool. Some milkmaid in Ireland kicked it in the creek, I bet, and two months later here it comes round the Cape washing up to me. But you won't catch me doing any milking, no, sir—I ain't fooling with no cow's titties when I could be on down the road fooling with something else, don't you know?

For now, it's fishing for me, that and combing over this old beach and just, well, keeping an eye on things, like I need to be doing—keeping a lookout on those fools up in Hatteras Light, who can barely keep the damn thing lit. Coast Guard boys, now, they're all right, I'll give you that, and the navy radio guys, Doc Folb and them, they are too. But you wouldn't get a plug nickel out of me for any of them drawing government pay running Hatteras Light, not even one red Indian-head *cent*. Nothing.

All these folks wanting to know how come the *Carroll A. Deering* came smashing in here in plain sight of the lighthouse, well, hell, that's just it! Could've been there wasn't any light *to* see or the *Deering* would've seen it—how hard is that to figure out? Give me a federal job, put me up there in that light, now, and that old candle'd be outshining the sun—send everybody else on home, forget about shipwrecks out thisaway, cause there won't be any more of that business, now.

I know what goes on, don't think I don't, either. Why, just last week, I heard some of the boys talking, said that cutter—the one they keep down at Wilmington, *Seminole*—was coming back to blow up the *Carroll Deering* on account of they'd already salvaged her and stripped her and now she'd gone and broken in two and drifted off the shoals and was heading back out to the shipping lanes. Lord, I heard the noise this morning from way up north of the Cape, five times WHAM WHAM WHAM WHAM WHAM when they set her off. Bet nobody's heard anything like that since the Jerries mined the *Mirlo* back in the War and, hell, that's been three years.

And then what do I happen to see this morning when I'm down here, just checking on things? Look yonder, Mr. Christopher Columbus Gray, I says, who's this coasting down the way? Some kind of small craft all right, but I didn't spot any sails, now. Didn't make out any smoke, so how's she making her way?

Fool, says I to myself, she's just a part of that broken-up schooner, her bow by my lights cause I see the capstan. Just heading on down to somewhere the Lord only knows. And here I walked two miles of beach hoping maybe she'd take a turn and come on fetch up around here and I'd have a piece or two of her. It's always something you can find, make good use out of what washes up, even if it's nothing more'n some little old three-legged stool.

Sure, I stood there watching her till the breeze freshened and the waves picked up and she moved on out from this island and fell away and she's gone on down Ocracoke way, I expect, or even to Portsmouth Island. Somebody else'll have the better of her, instead of old C. C. Gray here.

It's all right—something'll turn up. Stuff's always drifting, and it's no telling, never, what might wash up. Way out here, something always does.

MUTINY ON THE *CITY OF ALTON*

Parish Prison
New Orleans, Louisiana
March 22, 1921

A quintet of *City of Alton* crewmen, four of them Russians, having tried and failed to organize a soviet aboard the steamship during its voyage from New York to Rio de Janeiro, were arrested by Brazilian police once the ship docked there. Loyal members of the *City of Alton*'s crew got the credit for putting down the revolution.

The American consul in Rio tried the five, ordering them back to the United States and shipping them north on the New York and Cuba line freighter *Rushville*, which had just made port at Rio to load coffee for New Orleans. The FBI met the ship in Louisiana, shackled the men hand and foot and hustled them in chains to the parish prison, treated them as desperadoes, and held them incommunicado.

They would stand trial in New York for mutiny on the high seas, and the Department of Justice would also investigate further the possibility that some or all of them—Bender, Kuobroozuff, Borsh, Randin, and Lipan—might somehow have been involved in the horrific Wall Street bombing of September 16, 1920.

MS FOUND IN A BOTTLE

Buxton Beach
Cape Hatteras, North Carolina
April 10, 1921

This was how Christopher Columbus Gray remembered it, how he told it later:

There were bottles in the surf and in the drift you disregarded and left alone, the fisherman thought, and then there were bottles you reached for, and this was one of the latter. Peculiar shaped, where'd it come from? No matter—it was what the corked bottle held that was worthy of wonder. The paper was wet—not dripping wet, but damp—coming out of the bottle, as Gray worked it out with a small stick.

Somehow it was not so soggy that it came apart. Gray turned that thought over and about in his mind before he ever took the first step with it back up the beach toward the liveoak woods and the small wooden house he kept with his wife and son.

The spring wind rattled the window lights—you couldn't keep anything tight down here, Gray thought. Not buildings, not boats. Not men, either. He considered again as he so frequently did that sorry crew running the lighthouse. Cape Hatteras Light, the biggest deal on the whole damn coast, he thought, and that sorry lot in there and him not, at least not *yet*, but they would see. C. C. Gray had three terms in the navy behind him, and he had put that on his application, sure he had. He'd get that job at the lighthouse yet, and when it came through he would deserve it.

Upon the rude unpainted table at home the fisherman laid the wet paper, unscrolled it, but then could scarcely make out the sloppy clots of penned words. He could hardly even differentiate ink from the body of the dark, watered sheet, though he tried.

Lord, what does it say?

Just let it be. Let it dry out. Couple of pine cones and a match in that tin heater and this place'll be hot enough for you, all right. Shanty hot, and dry as a Baptist church.

I know what the whole world wants to know, the fisherman reflected as the Grays' scant cottage warmed to the heater and the April morning. What's come of some people, that's all. Well, maybe I don't know *exactly* what happened, but with this paper here I can reckon what *might* of went with them, and maybe if I get it into the right hands everybody else can too.

So now let's see what it says:

Deering Captured by Oil Burning Boat
Something Like Chaser taking Off everything
Handcuffing Crew
Crew hiding All over Ship no Chance to
Make escape finder please
notify head Qtrs Of Deering

Fisherman Gray then sat down and wrote a short, important letter:

Buxton, N.C.
April 10, 1921

To U.S. Custom House
Norfolk, Va.

Dear Sir

If you know any thing of the Headquarters or owners of the six master Schooner *Carroll A. Deering* that came ashore on Diamonds Shoals I wish you would notify them that I have found a letter In a bottle on Cape Hatteras Beach telling how the ship came to be lost from one of the crew. For Information Concerning this letter write to me.

Christopher C. Gray
Buxton, N.C.

If necessary I can turn in my Discharges and recommendations to show my Honesty all along in the Navy. Hoping to here from this office real soon and many thanks for the Information.

Very Respectfully
Christopher Columbus Gray
Buxton, N.C.

On April 18, 1921, the U.S. Custom House in Norfolk stamped Gray's letter of alert duly RECEIVED.

LULA WORMELL
Portland, Maine
April 1921

Never before have I minded winter. How often—yes, sometimes even in winter—I used to take the jitney from Portland out to Cape Elizabeth and walk, picnic if the day were very fair, and watch with wonder the sea. How she pounded the rocks, as she has always and forever, and I could stand and gaze upon her till I were near *hypnotized*, my friends always said. We have to drag you away, Lula, they said.

Well, then, so be it. I love the strength and the soul of it, and to me every magnificent pounding wave and spray from it is a message from Father, yes, like a wave of his hand, a vigorous precursor of his return. Think nothing unusual of this—for everyone who has family at sea must make some sort of peace with her, must have some way of seeing her that is not hostile. We must believe the sea that takes our loved ones away from us is the same sea that will bring them safely home again.

We must.

Strange of me, perhaps, that I have kept going down from Portland to the Cape, even after the *Deering* came in with no one aboard. If there were hypnosis involved, it would have been *I* who was seeking to charm the sea—oh, yes, I thought this wildly, crazily—to charm her and make her produce Father, or send us some word of him. And who's to say my chants and prayers have not worked?

So I could have kissed that man Gray, just outright hugged his neck and kissed him in front of God and the world. For that moment when the Deerings' word reached us about his having found a note in a bottle, I felt like he had found Father. How many people would have stopped to pick up an old bottle in the surf? And then, seeing wet paper inside, how many would have done any more with it than just drop it, or throw it back?

Oh, to think he might have thrown it back.

But his name—look at his name: Christopher Columbus Gray. Others may laugh at my fondness for this man I have never met, but there is in his very name a sense of discovery. And that is what he did, discovered Father.

What a thin thread we all hang upon and hold to life by. Mr. Gray who spends his life in an open boat upon great waters—for he is a fisherman, they tell me—upon the sound or the seas, might well not have chosen to spend his idle hour that day in a stroll upon the shore. Might well not have plucked that odd little bottle up when he saw it. Might well not have carried the vessel and its damp contents home with him and taken care with it that we here in Portland should have word of Father, if not his whereabouts, the first word in ten weeks!

Now people will know what has been happening off our shore.

Not just people at the Deering office in Bath, but important people in the capital. It's just Barbary pirates all over again, perhaps worse. If they learn in Washington who and what nation is sponsoring these pirates, I wouldn't be surprised if America goes to war. I really wouldn't.

So of course I say I could've kissed Mr. Gray. I would've, too, had I been there, and would only wish my kiss were reward enough, for he is a hero to me.

I hope Congress gives him a medal.

MORE TROUBLE FOR THE DEERINGS
Nassau, Bahamas
May 5, 1921

The five-masted schooner *Gardiner G. Deering* lay at anchor in Nassau, with First Mate Walter Matthews in command and wiring the Deerings back in Bath what had occurred on the high seas between Barbados and this Bahamian port.

Captain Chester T. Wallace of Bath, a man who had spent fifty of his sixty-two years at sea, went insane and was then shot and killed by the ship's cook in self defense. Wallace, a well-known mariner and exceptional navigator who had commanded the schooners *Oliver S. Barrett*, *Helen Crosby*, and *Ada F. Brown* and the *Edward J. Lawrence*, which craft he brought back to America from Amsterdam during the Great War, now lay dead.

The first mate, just then being deposed by the U.S. consul in Nassau, wrote in his cablegram that there was no mutiny on board, that all was quiet, and that he was prepared to bring the ship on home with the present crew, all of whom besides himself were black.

What were the Deerings to make of this latest tragic dispatch? Could no ship bearing their name on her stern and nameboards make it back from Brazil and Barbados anymore without trouble?

LULA WORMELL

57 Lawn Avenue
Portland, Maine
May 1921

Where on earth has this message come from?

It is supposed to be a wireless from the steamer *Hewitt*, and is said to have made it to Mother on the 7th of February—but I know she never received it. She never saw it—neither of us did!—till the man from the *Portland Evening Express* called at Lawn Avenue today and showed it to us. I must leave Portland at once, as there is so much yet to do. I must go to Washington, and, too, there is much to inquire about in Norfolk—Carlson, the wrecking tug captain, has agreed to see me and discuss the state the *Carroll A. Deering* was in when he boarded and inspected her back in February. If anything could've bolstered Mother's and my firm belief that Father and the *Deering*'s crew are yet alive, seeing this mysterious message has done that, for it read:

Meade: Safe. Willis.

Almeda Case Allen was my mother's maiden name. Meade is the name Father calls Mother by.

No one else in the world uses it.

HANDWRITING (I)

Portland, Maine
May 22–24, 1921

In Milton, Delaware, Captain George Goodwin of the *Brooks* had taken a moment to compose a short letter to Lula Wormell, a few kind words to her from one of her father's peers. He told her he had heard from Captain Wormell when they were together in Rio that the *Deering*'s mate was worthless, the bos'n not much better. But Goodwin had known Engineer Herbert Bates for years, and he was satisfied, he said, that Bates "would stick by Captain Wormell should anything out of the ordinary occur. It is hard to realize the constant strain on your

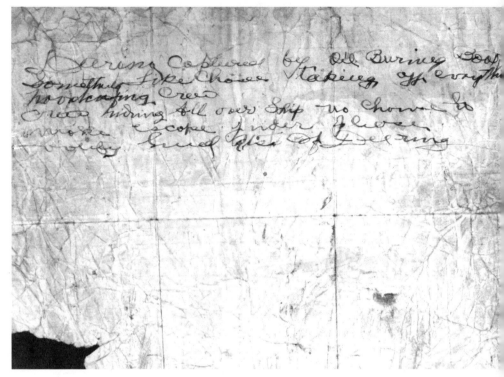

The bottle letter Christopher Columbus Gray reported finding in April 1921 on the beach at Buxton, near Cape Hatteras, N.C.

Mother and you these last few months, but it must be a relief to you both knowing he was a good Christian man."

Yes, it was a relief, and it was a comfort, too, to Lula Wormell when she received Captain Goodwin's note. And her subsequent receipt of three handwriting analyses in quick succession was a real jolt of hope and good fortune, for they read:

Portland, Maine
May 23d, 1921
To whom it may concern:
 I have carefully compared the writing of the original message picked up in a bottle by Mr. Gray of Buxton, North Carolina, with

Rio de Janeiro Brazil 4/30/20

Dear Mother Just a few lines this morning to say Hello. expect to finish discharging today and will Probaly go to sea Dec 2d. we are going to Barbados for Orders. will Probaly go to Norfolk from there. dont know yet. I was on board the schr Governor Brooks. Sunday and had dinner she is in here in distress been here six months I sprained my ankle there Sunday and I am all most a Cripple since. its not very painful only swollen very baddy. guess I will be alright in a few days I havent much work to do for a few days so will not have to stand up very much. I dread the Cold weather but will be in it in about six weeks I expect I havent seen any American newspapers since being here. Therefore I dont know any news. Thats all for now. you Can see in the paper where the schr is going from barbados if to Hampton Roads Va you Can write me in Care of Carroll A. Deering to Clarke Tow Boat Company
Norfolk Va
hope these few lines will find you making out alright Love from Herb

The letter *Carroll A. Deering* engineer Herbert Bates wrote home from Rio de Janeiro, Brazil, November 1920 the signature on the ship's papers and the letter signed Herb, said to be the last one written by the engineer of the Sch. *Carroll Deering*, Mr. Herbert Bates. I find quite a strong similarity, and it is my opinion that the writing in question *was* written by the same hand. I have examined the signature of the entire ship's crew and find only this one giving any similarity in the handwriting.

Respectfully,

Ralph E. Rowe

Supervisor of Penmanship & Drawing

Portland Public Schools.

Portland, Maine

May 24th, 1921

Comparison of letters and words showing similarity of form and habits in two letters known as the "Bottle Letter," and what may be designated as the "Rio Letter," dated at Rio de Janeiro, hereafter referred to as—B.L. and RIO L.

In the B.L. there are ten capitals as follows:—D.C.O.B.S., L.T.A.G. and Q. In the RIO L. all of the above appear once or more except the G. and Q.

Taking them in order of their appearance on the B.L. the capital D has a characteristic loop alike in each case.

The capital C has a full curve alike in all and in the words "captured" and "crew" corresponds with the C in the word "Company" in the RIO L. in that it joins with the small letters in same word. As a rule the capital does not join with the small o following.

The capital O in Oil in the B.L. is quite like the O in "Orders" in the RIO L.

The capital B in "Burning" and in "Boat" in B.L. is of same general style as the B in the RIO L. especially in the loop which connects with the small letter following. See words "Brooks" and "Boat," in RIO L.

The capital S in B.L. in words "Something" and "Ship" are identical in almost every feature with the capital S in "Schr." in the RIO L.

The capital L in "Like" in B.L. compared with the L in "Love" at bottom of RIO L. will show similarity.

The capital T in B.L. (if it is meant for a capital), is so like the capital T in word "Tow" and in word "That" and "Therefore" that one cannot help being impressed with its strong similarity. This is not very common in use as a capital except in printing.

In the small r the shoulder part is almost exactly alike in the two letters for comparison.

Perhaps more noticeable still is the similarity in the small "k." Look at this letter in the word "Like" and in the word "make" on the B.L. and compare it with the same letter wherever it occurs in the RIO L. Now compare the small k in word "taking" with the word "know" in the RIO L. on the 16th line.

Note the beginning of the small b in word "by" in B.L. with the same letter wherever it is used as an initial letter in the RIO L.

The habit of terminating a word with a downward stroke may be observed as common to both by comparing the e in "please" in B.L. with the words "much work" on the 12th line of the RIO L.

The crowding of words and of letters in a word shows a habit common to both.

The variation in the slant of letters in the same word may be noticed by comparing word "Burning" and "every thing" in the B.L. with similar words in the RIO L.

There are many other similarities either in individual letters or in spacing and slant of letters and words all of which tend to the conclusion that one person wrote them both.

H. W. Shaylor,

Supervisor Writing in the Portland Pub. Schools. 1870 to 1915.

Portland, Maine

May 24th, 1921

Dear Mrs. Wormell,

Having examined the original unsigned note which was picked up in a bottle, describing the trouble on board the Schooner *Deering*, and having also examined the original signatures of the Schooner's crew, as well as the letter, said to have been the last written by Engineer Herbert Bates, while in South America, to his mother at home, I find many points of similarity in the acknowledged hand-writing of the said Engineer Herbert Bates, and the unsigned note to which I have above referred. That the note was written by Engineer Bates, under the trying circumstances described, seems altogether reasonable.

Sincerely yours,
Elmer S. Moody,
Formerly Proprietor of the
Moody School of Shorthand & Business

The assumption of all three analysts was that the Bottle Letter was genuine, and that the question quite literally at hand was straight and simple: who from among the *Carroll A. Deering*'s crew was the author of the note? The three reports that reached Lawn Avenue gave no doubt of either the document's authenticity or its authorship—Chief Engineer Herbert Pillsbury Bates.

When the first of these reports came to her on May 23, Lula Wormell, accompanied by Captain "Hungry Bill" Merritt, traveled immediately up the Maine coast to Bath, to the Washington Street offices of the G. G. Deering Company, where she met the brothers Harry and Carroll Deering of the firm.

Harry G. Deering let her know straightaway that he had very little faith in a congressional investigation's coming up with the solution of the *Deering* mystery, with the ascertainment and apprehension of modern pirates, or with the safe return of the schooner's crew.

"Won't you come to Washington with us?" Miss Wormell implored him.

"No," said Harry Deering flatly. "I won't."

But the bookkeeper Carroll A. Deering himself was not so dismissive of Lula Wormell's notions as was his brother Harry. "Why, twentieth-century pirates might have an excellent opportunity to work," he said, "by buying up naval craft that was recently sold off, and they might carry on piracy for a long time—undisturbed—because of the general belief that piracy is extinct."

In some backward way Mr. Deering's logic buoyed the captain's

Carroll Atwood Deering, bookkeeper, G. G. Deering Company, Bath, Maine

daughter—for though it was speculative word, it was solidly delivered. That the very outlandishness of the piracy idea was in fact the best shield or disguise the filibustering pursuit might possess gave Lula Wormell a great hope.

Though he had no belief in the possibility of her mission's success,

Harry Deering was willing at least to write and sign for her a letter of support from the Deering Company:

To whom it may concern:—

We understand that the bearer of this, Miss Lula Wormell, daughter of Capt. Wormell, is going to Washington to see if she can get any information from any source in regard to what can be done to throw any light on the matter, and any assistance that can be given her by anybody will be appreciated by the members of this concern, as on account of sickness and business no member of this concern is able to accompany her.

Back in Portland the next day, the second and third handwriting analyses arrived. An informal fourth report corroborating the three studies was that of Captain Merritt, who also compared the Bottle Letter with Engineer Bates's letter home from Rio, and who told the *Portland Evening Express*:

"I was well acquainted with Bates. I knew his writing and its characteristics. You see, he had a peculiarity of dropping in a capital letter now and then in his writings—just where there was no need of one. He would use a capital letter in spelling some little word—"

"Half way in a sentence?" the *Express* man asked.

"Exactly," said Captain Merritt. "That same thing occurred in the note and I am at a loss to account for anyone, not familiar with his way of writing, to fake a note such as this."

Lula Wormell had all the evidence she needed. So armed, she would now go to Washington, D.C., and there make her case.

LULA WORMELL
Portland, Maine
Late May 1921

This is not what I wanted to do—or expected to.

To analyze handwritings, to speak with reporters whether friendly or rude, on streets and on railway platforms—to bother and in my case I might say *badger*, in turn, my preacher, my senator, and

Lord knows who all in Washington including bless his heart that man who (some say even now) may one day be our president, Mr. Herbert Hoover.

We have proof—*proof!*—I tell you. We have writing in all their hands, the seamen's from their articles when they had signed on with the *Deering* in Norfolk late last summer, the mate's from Delaware when he came on with Father, and the engineer's—that was Henry Bates—writing from a letter he'd sent his mother over in Islesboro, here in Maine.

We have the note Mr. Gray found at Buxton Beach (can you believe the *New York Times* called it Buckstone Beach?), got it sent up in April from the Norfolk Custom House, through the Coast Guard, we did. And we showed that note to not one, not two, but *three* experts in handwriting, and all of them agreed—the writing on the Buxton note was identical to that in the letter Mrs. Bates had sent us.

Somehow Henry Bates managed to write that note and thank God he did and how he ever got away with it with pirates aboard the ship to get it into that bottle and throw it overboard in time, I do not know. But he did, and I'll say again, God bless Christopher Columbus Gray for finding it and taking such care with it.

So yes, I've importuned our preacher, and Captain Merritt, and Senator Hale—I only wish the Deerings whose name is on that ship would come to Washington with us, but with or without them, I am going. And if I had to, I would go alone.

Just tell me who else would've lifted enough of a hand to make something happen?

If not the captain's daughter, who else?

I knew, I swear I tell you, I *knew* from the first, when the telegram came and Mother sitting in the parlor crying and through all of it I knew that it would wind up falling to me. Mother, she's worried over every clue that's come our way, and she's worked herself sick over it all. To begin with, she always hated the ocean—and I don't know how she could even put her mind on any of this, let alone keep it there. Well, let me be her agent then, to act out her will, but, Lord, don't let anyone think any the less of her. That's just her way, how she's lived with Father being gone, being out there at sea, for most all their lives together. Together.

From everyone I have heard the talk and I tell you it does sound convincing, about the sailorman's prerogative. Distant ports of call and women, wanton and waiting, in them all. Romantic, they call it, but I call them rogues for saying so. If you asked my mother she would tell you—what is the romance of the sea for such as she, a woman waiting, too, but one devoted and faithful? Two words and two only:

Widow's walk.

Bitter, am I? Am I not? Father was retired, and powerful lucky to have gone this distance—sixty-six years—and now still to be here, with his own family, vacationing on our own grand coast, when they called him. Why did he go, and why on earth did we let him?

My God, Gard Deering—you could've found a younger man, or any other man. Father was great with the sea, yes, great with sailing, we knew that—everyone did. Of all the captains you might've sent to Delaware to carry the *Deering* on, why did you call ours?

Doesn't matter now, Mother. Still, a woman can't help but wonder. Can't help.

Can't help but wonder.

Can't . . . .

CHRISTOPHER COLUMBUS GRAY

Buxton Beach
Cape Hatteras, North Carolina
Late Spring 1921

Anybody can blink a damn light.

Way you do something in this world is find the truth and tell somebody about it. Way you get ahead, like get a better job.

So I've been fishing, and that's a hard way to serve the Lord, I tell you what.

I could work a lighthouse better than those fools there now. I know it. What's there to it but climbing a bunch of damn spiral stairsteps and keep a wick trimmed and a fire to it? Good an eye as I've got, you think I couldn't keep up with such as that? I don't miss a thing, you ask anybody. Walk this beach is what I do—you can't ever tell what'll come to you, that's the way of it out here.

But you can't sit just in a house and go up and set a light to blinking and think that's doing anything. You've got to pay more attention than that and get out and see what it is—see what's really going on, like I do.

Out here on this beach, it'll come to you.

You take when that tanker *Mirlo* hit the mines and went down. All those men in the water and the water on fire and I'm thinking, could it be any worse than *that*? Then for days after they sank her when I'd go down to the ocean after high tide'd turned, here there'd be these dark little lines one right after the next going back down into the water, oil lines that the tide had left there, going out. Like the devil himself'd drug his fingertip right along the sand time and time again till the whole beach was just drawn and nothing else was down there but those lines of death.

Well, not everybody's going be there to pull a man out of the burning oil, like Cap'n John Midgett was. And I'm not taking a thing away from him and his men, either—hell, they pulled forty men or more out of the drink that night, and the Brits didn't lose but ten, I think. Those boys from Chicamacomico Station was heroes, all of em. But there's some of us got to be here on shore when something like, say, a bottle washes up. That ought to mean something, count for something, oughtn't it?

Yes, sir, captain, I reckon it oughta.

LULA WORMELL
57 Lawn Avenue
Portland, Maine
Late May 1921

What do I wear to meet Senator Hale? What, indeed, to wear to meet the Secretary of Commerce? Or of State?

And what do I say?

Of course a girl from Maine must find her missing father, but they will tell me—as others have right here in Portland—that there are young women everywhere who have lost fathers and brothers and sweethearts in the War and that I am hardly alone in this. Everyone *must* be reunited with those they love, and of course everyone would have it that way, but I know this will not come to pass. I know there are men—and boys—buried at Flanders whose identities, even the facts of whose deaths, will never be known.

That is at the heart of what I cannot stand, for myself, and for Mother. And I will not.

I cannot solve the mysteries of their loved ones for all those widows and sisters and parents, for all those girlfriends, but I can help Mother and me. And I can help Father—and who else *would* help him more than his own flesh and blood? He would tell me, don't forget who you are, sugar, or where you come from, who your people are, and he would ask me to keep my head clear and my wits about me and be sensible, practical, forthright and, above all, always honest. The way he was, and *is* yet, somewhere, I know—

Lord, I do know.

Well, leave it to this librarian to be systematic, if nothing else—I must write down my points, so I can set them out and not get flustered or confused. Far more important to be clear and firm with what Mother and I have learned these last weeks than overworry about what I should wear to meet our leaders.

Very well, then—paper, pen, ink, and my points:

Six reasons why I believe the stranding of the *Deering* was due to unnatural causes . . .

First—The weather was good both the day preceding and on the day of the wreck. Government reports from Coast Guard stations in that vicinity and also a letter from a sea captain, who was in about the same position as the *Deering*, verify the statement that on January 29 and 30 (Saturday and Sunday) the weather was fine. There had been a storm the 25th, 26th, and 27th, but it was all over before the *Deering* struck and it was not of unusual severity while it lasted. There was at the time of the accident no storm, no fog, no wind, other than that designated as a moderate breeze. Nothing whatever to justify the wrecking of a big schooner like the *Deering*.

Second—The condition in which the vessel was left was questionable. The fact that the schooner was left with all sails set seemed queer, for it indicated no attempt was ever made by lowering top sails and jibs and lowering other sails, to save her. Any experienced captain would naturally have done these things as soon as he found his ship in danger. Also, something about the condition of the cabin seemed rather strange and the fact that a sledgehammer was found on deck near the steering gear attracted attention. It looked as if it might have been used to break the steering gear so that the rudder would swing free and the vessel would more easily drift with the current. This would indicate that the schooner had been abandoned before grounding and purposely left to drift on shoal.

Third—There was never the slightest trace of any wreckage found. Of course, the wind and current right, such things might drift out to sea, yet with all things like clothing, grips, papers, etc., taken, and considering the facts that sailors are none too good packers at best and how closely the vessel and surrounding waters were watched and searched by Government agencies from the time she was first sighted, and also remembering that both lifeboats were of such construction as not to be easily swamped, one would be justified in expecting some trace of wreckage to be seen.

Fourth—The crew was of a nationality that does not act rashly. The six sailors, the second mate, and possibly the first mate were Scandinavians—men who do not act hastily in time of accident—men trained from boyhood to know the nature of the surf and who would not be the kind to impulsively leave a vessel in the dark to go in lifeboats in an uncertain sea when it would be decidedly safer for them to remain on the ship until daylight at least.

Fifth—The captain did not give the message about the lost anchors when the *Deering* passed Lookout Shoal lightship at 4:30 P.M., January 29th. Considering the extremely genial temperament of Captain Wormell, it would have been natural to expect that he either would have given this message himself or, if on deck standing by the men at the wheel, as has been suggested, he would in some way have saluted the captain of the lightship.

Sixth—A steamer which passed the Lookout lightship after the *Deering* would not stop even on the second signal for the message the captain of the lightship wished to give out about the *Deering* having lost her anchors. The lightship's wireless was out of order, but the captain tried to attract attention of the steamer both by using an international code signal and by blasts of her chime whistle which could be heard five miles. Contrary to the unwritten law of the sea, the steamer would not stop or answer the lightship's signals.

There, now.

As if that mightn't be enough, then, beyond all this there is Mr. Gray's bottle, and Engineer Bates's note from within it. Let the newspapers call me the "dauntless daughter" and the "soul of the search" and so be it. Father always—*always!*—kept his faith with me, and as God is my witness I will keep my faith with him.

The tips of the treebranch outside keep tapping the windowlights, and I can hear the foghorn bellowing way off down in the harbor, a low and lonesome sound, and maybe there's a moaning in it, too, or maybe I'm just hearing things.

Mother is rattling around down the hall, worrying about it all, opening and closing her door too much—she said this afternoon down in the kitchen that just the thought of my trip makes her want to take to her bed. Not me—my eyes are tired but my heart is light as spring air about Washington, because this trek is something we must do and because we must, I want to. Who can imagine sitting home doing nothing?

Pack, Lula! It's almost midnight, and, though I'm traveling to the District of Columbia, I am not *moving* there—so how can a steamer trunk full of bloomers and skirts weigh so much, pray? If only I could fit it all into my little Sears traveling case . . . such a comfort, one's dearest things all tucked away just so in moire linen (that's why I bought it, that lining)—my ivory white comb, my Siberian bristle brush, the linen's rolled pattern peering out, watery, and how like waves.

Like waves.

What should I wear? And why must it be so hard to decide, when there's everything else in the world to think about?

My hat! Where are you, hat! Oh, there, how'd you get over there? No matter—stay here, hat, on my little russet case. Brass lock, brass key, close case. And be ready in the morning, all.

To bed, now.

To Washington tomorrow, then, and wearing your hat, Lula. Never without a hat!

ENGAGING HERBERT HOOVER

Herbert Clark Hoover came to the southern city on the Potomac as President Harding's secretary of commerce, and he and his wife Lou Henry moved into a big brick bungalow at 2300 S Street NW, its acre of garden wanting care. She would take on the tangles and overgrowth and set it to right, and on the large back porch they would dine and entertain and aim someday for a different address, one on Pennsylvania Avenue. Their neighbor just down the street at 2340 was Woodrow Wilson, the former president who only four years earlier had put Hoover in charge of the Food Administration, with which Hoover had then gone on to feed Belgium, the Allies, and the starving hordes of Europe.

Now the Hoovers of S Street were so close to the top.

Yet Hoover balanced upon a thin wire, and a high one—without the aid of a net. So imbued with both the humanity of relief and the logistical expertise to deliver it, Hoover was heroically impelled to feed the Russians.

All the flame-fanners of the Red Scare were against him. One of the leaders of the National Civic Federation had already warned the nation that sixty thousand Bolshevik sympathizers were somehow in on, or behind, the work of the Russian Famine Fund Committee. Sixty thousand! Even the national League of Women Voters was suspect. Even the names of Charlie Chaplin and Will Rogers showed up in Communist files, and mere mention therein was enough to raise millions of

Lula Wormell of Portland, Maine

American eyebrows, to set millions of patriotic tongues a-wagging about show business and moral laxity and about how the little tramp and the cowboy philosopher might well be the thin end of the revolutionary wedge. Today vaudeville and the movies, tomorrow Charlie Trotsky and Will Lenin.

When the social workers from a rainbow of agencies appeared in Washington that summer and met en masse to coordinate the Russian relief, one woman rose to criticize the very idea, saying directly to Hoover, "Mr. Secretary, aren't we going to help Bolshevism by feeding these people?"

But the Russians were beset by drought and had nothing left of last year's harvest and were eating grass cakes and grass soup, having finished off all their dogs and cats and the very bark off the trees, and feed them he would. To this thrust Hoover parried noisily, leaping to his feet and banging the table before him as he shouted:

"Twenty million people are starving—whatever their politics, they shall be fed!"

Herbert Hoover would bull on through, and in short order (after he successfully offered the Russians food in exchange for the release of American prisoners) would hear the gratitude of a prostrate people. In one instance it came from no less than Maxim Gorky, the noted novelist and playwright (and friend of Chekhov and Tolstoy, though also of Lenin), who wrote to one American woman, saying, "Never before has any one country come to the relief of another with such generosity and such munificence of resources and means—America has a right to be proud of her children who are so splendidly toiling on the vast fields of death, in an environment of epidemics, barbarization, and cannibalism."

But Hoover would aid no Bolshevik buccaneers in the process, most especially those who might be prowling the Graveyard of the Atlantic, kidnapping—*impressing*—our sailors and putting them to toil before the mast of Mother Russia. If somehow Bolshevik pirates were really making off with any portion of the American merchant marine, at the same time Hoover was putting food upon their people's very plates, and Hoover were to commit anything less than the full measure of his department's power to stopping it, well . . . there would be no president-in-the-making that way.

When it came time to honor the request of Maine's Republican senator Frederick Hale and meet some of his people from Down East, Hoover was more than willing to comply. The secretary of commerce had every reason in the world to want to find the *Deering*'s crew; he had the interests of the Deering family at heart, and those of the Wormells, and, last and strongest, he very much had his own.

LULA WORMELL AT COMMERCE

Department of Commerce
19th Street and Pennsylvania Avenue, NW
Washington, D.C.
Late May 1921

The steam train left Portland for points south, and Lula Wormell found herself leading a delegation that now also included the Reverend Doctor Addison Benjamin Lorimer, pastor at the Central Square Baptist Church and the Wormells' near-neighbor at 36 Lawn Avenue, as well as the original master of the *Carroll A. Deering*, Captain "Hungry Bill" Merritt.

In Washington, D.C., this party met with Senator Hale from Portland, who directed them to the Commerce Department, for it was Commerce that ran the lightships and lighthouses, Commerce that ran the coast. Surely if there were help to be had, they would find it there, so Hale called ahead, advancing an introduction, and in short order — after they had first seen the commissioner of navigation and convinced him of the validity of their case and Lula Wormell had placed her name and address on file — the threesome walked into the office of the secretary himself, Herbert Clark Hoover.

The compact engineer in the dark double-breasted serge suit was seated behind his desk. His stiff shirt collar was rounded, his short hair center-parted. To his right stood a Tiffany lamp, the black telephone on its stand to his left. Hoover rose briskly and nodded good-days, shaking hands with the preacher and the sea captain, then reseated

Secretary of Commerce Herbert Clark Hoover

himself. They were awed by his presence, too much so to converse for a moment.

"I understand from Senator Hale," the secretary began, "that you have already done quite a lot of work on this case, Miss Wormell."

"Mr. Hoover," Lula Wormell said. "Mr. Hoover, my father is alive.

He is alive somewhere on the Atlantic Ocean and I know he is and though I know I cannot find him, I know you can. With the navy. With the Coast Guard. Some wild bunch has captured him—don't ask me why they would do such a thing—Lord knows, a sea captain's family could pay no ransom."

From a large envelope she withdrew her *Six Points*, her copies of the memoranda drafted by the three Portland handwriting experts, each one confirming the *Deering* engineer Herbert Bates's authorship of the bottle letter, identifying each piece for him. She stood and strode to his desk and laid the proof down on the blotter before him, and said,

"I have longed to come to Washington all my life and see its wonders, but all I want now is to be back in Portland, with my father at the head of the table smiling and presiding over the carving of a roast beef and telling us, Mother and me, once again, *we shall not want—*"

Secretary Hoover leaned toward her, stared into her eyes, taken by her energy and by the clarity of her speech. By her fundamental forthrightness, he would later recall to others. Hoover heard in her voice as penetrating an appeal as any ever tendered to him. He watched her as intently as she did him, as she stepped backward now, not a bit awkwardly, and took her seat again between her pastor and the old mariner. Hoover studied and scanned the sheaf she had given him, and over a minute passed before he uttered a sound. Both Senator Hale and Hoover's own staff at Commerce had given him the *Deering*'s particulars, but Lula Wormell's work now substantially increased the common, working knowledge of the case. Hoover needed nothing more. The brief interview might have been only a courtesy to Hale, had Herbert Hoover not met with such an earnest and moving—and *informed*—force as Lula Wormell.

The secretary of commerce rose and clasped his hands behind his back.

"We can help you, Miss Wormell," he said. "We can and we will. I intend to involve every federal agency that may prove useful to this search and to the solution of the mystery. This business with the *Deering* is not only baffling—it may already involve a breach in our national security. As of today I will have an excellent man—Lawrence Richey—working on this and reporting directly to me. If it is humanly possible to make it be so, you shall have your father back."

Hoover had yet another cause, Lula Wormell had a champion, and now it would all be just a matter of time. This much comfort the small party of seekers could take with them back home to Maine.

"You shall have your father back," Hoover had told her, and she believed him; she added to his six words five of her own and now she had herself a litany: *Just a matter of time.*

DEPARTMENT OF STATE
Washington, D.C.
June 2, 1921

The impact of Lula Wormell's visit to Washington was enormous and immediate. In less than a week Henry Fletcher, Undersecretary of State and one of the officials she and her party had met with, had drafted a "proposed instruction" that, once approved by Hoover's people in Commerce, would go all over the world, to wit:

The Honorable The Secretary of Commerce
Sir: Attention of the Commissioner of Navigation
    I have the honor to enclose for your consideration and comment a copy of a proposed instruction to all Consular Officers at Seaports relative to the wreck of the American schooner *Carroll A. Deering*. This instruction is being forwarded at the request of the daughter of Captain Wormell, master of the vessel, who is understood to have brought the matter to the attention of the Department of Commerce.
    Before sending the instruction, I shall be pleased if you will furnish to the Department of State an expression of your views regarding it.
    I have the honor to be, Sir,
Your obedient servant,

For the Secretary of State:
Henry P. Fletcher
Under Secretary

To the American Consular Officers at Seaports
Gentlemen:

On January 29th, 1921, the American schooner *Carroll A. Deering*, sailing at the rate of about five miles per hour, passed Cape Lookout Light Ship, North Carolina, and on January 31st, 1921, it was found a few miles north of that point in such condition that there is every suspicion of foul play having occurred. The vessel cleared for Norfolk, Virginia, from Rio de Janeiro and put into Barbados for orders, but, receiving no different orders, proceeded on its voyage to Norfolk. After passing Cape Lookout Light Ship, the vessel was not again seen until it was found as a wreck and nothing has been heard from the members of the crew. The master of the vessel, Captain Wormell, is reported to have been experienced as a navigator and thoroughly reliable.

At the time the *Carroll A. Deering* passed the Cape Lookout Light Ship, a man on board, other than the Captain, hailed the Light Ship and reported that the vessel had lost both anchors and asked to be reported to his owners. Otherwise the vessel appeared to be in very good condition. A short time after the schooner passed the Light ship, a steamer, the name of which can not be ascertained, which was passing, was asked to stop and take a message for forwarding, and in spite of numerous attempts on the part of the master of the Light Ship to attract the vessel's attention, no response to his efforts was received.

On April 11, 1921, the following message was picked up in a bottle near Cape Hatteras:

DEERING CAPTURED BY OIL BURNING BOAT SOMETHING LIKE CHASER TAKING OFF EVERYTHING HANDCUFFING CREW HIDING ALL OVER SHIP NO CHANCE TO MAKE ESCAPE FINDER PLEASE NOTIFY HEADQUARTERS OF DEERING.

Inasmuch as the Navy Department has recently disposed of a number of subchasers, it is thought that the reference in the message may be to one of those vessels which has been taken over by unprincipled persons who may now be using it as a raider.

The *Carroll A. Deering* carried a motor lifeboat and a dory, but neither of them has been picked up and no wreckage from them has been found. All the provisions, clothing, and supplies of the vessel had been removed.

A description of Captain Wormell, master of the *Carroll A. Deering*, follows.

You are instructed to make discreet inquiries and investigate carefully any clues which may lead to the discovery of the crew of the *Carroll A. Deering* and an explanation of the disaster. If you succeed in finding out anything which may lead to the discovery of the crew, you will telegraph the Department at once giving full details. Negative information need not be reported.

I am, Gentlemen,

Your obedient servant,

For the Secretary of State:

LULA WORMELL

Washington, D.C.

Early June 1921

Oh, what a place this is, more marble, I'm sure of it, than we've got in the whole state of Maine! Would that it's done some good for us to all traipse down here and ride streetcars from one end of Pennsylvania Avenue to the other and knock on all these dark enormous doors.

Such courtesy and kindness we've been met with, it amazes me, considering how apparently wild was our theory! Why, we've gone from the Commerce Department to the Justice Department, the State Department, we've met Mr. Reynolds, the commandant of the Coast Guard, and we've even seen Teddy Roosevelt Junior who's the assistant secretary of the navy!

Reverend Lorimer gave me his copy of the *Washington Times* and said "Go on, read all about it—you've caused quite a stir in this old town." My word, I could scarcely believe they were talking about me, but there I was, the "nervy and sturdy young Maine girl" being of "invaluable aid to the various Government agencies who are investigating the sea mystery." They even said I had "remarkable detective abilities." The female Sherlock Holmes, from Down East Maine, am I now?

Oh, would that it'll all add up to something, like Mr. Hoover said it would. The days keep going by so fast, so many of them. Far too many of them. But now men are looking all over the world, aren't they? God bless them, merciful heavens, and Godspeed.

Reverend Lorimer and I are away to Norfolk now, to see what of the trail we might pick up there. So God bless us, too.

WORD FROM THE BATES FAMILY
Pripet, Maine
June 6, 1921

Dear Mrs. Wormell:—
Mother feels that the clue which the bottle message gives us is a most tangible one. My brother Herbert is a very cool headed man in time of stress—also ingenious. He always carried his fountain pen with him, no matter in what clothes he was dressed. Also he believed in many of the old customs of sea life that many now consider "gone by."

We are most sincerely hoping and praying that you may be in time to help our dear ones and bring them back safely to us, but even if you are not, an investigation by the government may help to lessen danger to others in the days and years to come. For it certainly seems that piracy is lifting its head in an age of civilization that will not tolerate it.

You may rest assured that no publicity will be given this matter until you deem it safe and wise.

Very sincerely yours,
Beulah Bates Williams

FIND THESE MEN

Bureau of Navigation
Washington, D.C.
June 7, 1921

From the commissioner of navigation's office came a directive to the shipping commissioners at Portland, San Francisco, Seattle, Los Angeles, and Honolulu to scour their records, all crew lists and shipping articles, in an attempt to discover the whereabouts, present addresses, names, and addresses of next of kin, *anything* about the seamen of the *Carroll A. Deering*.

Oddly, though, the directive did not ask for such information on *all* the *Deering*'s crew, listing only McLellan, Nielsen, Jensen, Olsen, and Frederickson—half the crew. And one member, the mate McLellan, appeared on the directive's list as *Cyril*, though the first mate's name was Charles. For one Cyril McLellan, the trail warmed, slightly, briefly, intriguingly—he had gotten himself able-bodied seaman's papers in Portland, Oregon, in late March 1921, but merely gave his address as that of the local sailors' union. But there was no record of his ever shipping out of Portland, nor any of his turning up anywhere in any fashion, from the Pacific Northwest on down to the coast of California. It was as if he had appeared only for the purpose of disappearing, like a man who almost never was.

And however incomplete was the roll that went out, the responses coming back to Washington from the West Coast added nothing but mystery to it, as the word from Special Deputy Collector Mahan, U.S. Customs Service, Port of Los Angeles, exemplified:

"Careful inspection fails to disclose any information regarding any of the seamen mentioned. The Secretary of the Sailors' Union at this port has no record of these seamen."

No record.

LULA WORMELL

Home of Mrs. DeWitt Masterson
822 Potomac Avenue
Buffalo, New York
June 12, 1921

What to write Mr. Richey, after all this traveling: that the bottle-message paper was Norwegian, did I say that already?

In Norfolk I went to six paper companies, and none of them had ever handled any such as I described the note's being written on, *without* vertical lines and *with* narrow spacing and heliotrope or light purple inking. At last I was referred to Captain Williams of Henry Kessel and Company, considered an authority on foreign paper, and he thought it might have been imported from Scandinavia and bought in Brazil. In Washington there are experts in paper, and they, too, said it was made in Norway and was of a pattern and sort a good deal of which was shipped to South America.

And the bottle, that was made in Buenos Aires. Is it not all coming clear?

I know Mr. Bates, as engineer, had his own room near the sail-hoisting engine in the forecastle, and that one had to step down a step or two to get to it. Someone suggested, why, it might have been difficult for him, once he had written the note in his room, to have thrown that bottle through his porthole and up over the ship's rail.

Well, of course! Anything and everything might've been difficult— they were under attack, after all! The wonder 'tis not how he did it, but that he was able to do it at all.

While I was in Norfolk, I specifically wanted to see—and went to see—Captain Carlson of the wrecking tug *Rescue*, who was only on the *Deering* between 10:20 A.M. and 4:30 P.M. on February 4th and whose report I believe at best is more or less incomplete because of the haste involved. No trace of trouble or foul play were seen—but of course he wasn't looking for any, and, even had he been, any marks of this sort would have been obliterated by the washing of the sea!

As we went over what he had—and *hadn't*—found, Captain Carlson said that as regards the two missing anchors, there was no evidence to prove that they were not purposely "slipped" before the *Deering* passed the Lookout Shoals lightship and reported them gone. For the wrecking crew did not go down into the forward hold to ascertain if any chain were left in the locker—if anyone was in charge who should not have been and wanted to give the "lost anchors" report for a bluff, it could have been done.

Similarly, he had found the regular side lights in the rigging, and also two red lights that had been placed high in the rigging, one over the other—this signal is for either a wreck upon a beach or a vessel abandoned at sea, so it really tells us nothing. Of course, they could have been put there with the idea of deceiving, if one so desired.

And those boots in the little side room off Father's cabin, they don't make any sense! Not like Father's extremely orderly way for them to be left on the floor, especially at night—and why would the boots of other crew members have been in his quarters? They would not have, and that is that.

BODIES?
Washington, D.C.
June 16, 1921

Lawrence Richey had become an agent of the Secret Service when he was but sixteen, had done magazine and newspaper work in his twenties, and at thirty-two had gone to work as assistant office manager in Hoover's Food Administration during the Great War. He would serve Hoover as special assistant and secretary for many years— "the Hoover sleuth," H. L. Mencken would one day call him.

Richey put out an immediate request to the Bureau of Lighthouses: "I want all information re bodies of drowned persons washed ashore since January 25th last between New River Inlet and Bodie Island, North Carolina."

No mention of bodies, came the report that same day from Chief of

Lawrence Richey,
"the Hoover Sleuth"

Operations Maxam of the Coast Guard, who examined reports from the lifesaving stations over an even larger span of east coast from Charleston, South Carolina, to Cape May, New Jersey.

By July 11, the last of the lighthouses would answer the call. The keepers of both Ocracoke and Cape Lookout lights would advise that "they have not found any bodies nor heard of any being found by anyone in that vicinity."

Dead end.

SHIPPING THE BOTTLE

Central Square Baptist Church
Woodfords Station
Portland, Maine
June 16, 1921

The Coast Guard having sent Gray's drift bottle north from Norfolk to the Wormells in Portland, it remained in their possession during the month of June. Her mother wanted Lula to see it, but, upon learning that Lula would be detained in Buffalo, New York (where she had journeyed after Washington and Norfolk), for a few days more, Mrs. Wormell decided a photograph and a description of it would be enough for Lula to see and that she should ship it on at once, via Reverend Addison Lorimer, to Lawrence Richey in Washington.

In his letter to Mr. Richey, Reverend Lorimer, who was by now a most interested party in the *Deering* case, noted:

> The following facts have been obtained by Mrs. Wormell. Mr. Ralph Preble, connected with the H. H. Hay's Drug Company, this city, informs her that the bottle is unusual in the drug trade. He had never seen such. By consultation of catalogues he finds that such bottles are manufactured in Nova Scotia, in Philadelphia, in Baltimore, and in Buenos Ayres. The connection with South America may be in point.
>
> Hoping this may prove of some service in unravelling the mystery, and awaiting further advices from you,

I am very truly yours,
Addison B. Lorimer

LULA WORMELL

Home of Mrs. DeWitt Masterson
822 Potomac Avenue
Buffalo, New York
June 21, 1921

I must write Mr. Richey again.

Seven more spots I've gone to, here in Buffalo, looking for word about the bottle-note paper, and again the result is the same as it was in Norfolk. In no one of these has the buyer seen such paper inked in purple—all regular stock is *blue*.

And since I became aware of Miss Barbara Bauer's letters to the Coast Guard in Norfolk, I can't get her theory out of my mind. How this woman from Big Spring way out in west Texas knew the ship's captain of the *Hewitt*, a married man (and was familiar with his *handwriting*), Lord knows! But it hardly matters—she has seen a possible connection that none of the rest of us have.

Enemies of America, she thinks, took the men of the *Deering* after pursuing and somehow forcing the ship's grounding—the ship then useless, these enemies had to take the schooner's crew and then seek another ocean-going vessel to make their getaway, and that is where the *Hewitt* comes in. Off they go, perhaps toward Russia, or perhaps, she poses, toward the Gulf of Mexico somewhere.

For who shows up February 13th to attend two Bolshevik congresses in Mexico but Silvetzch and Landekoff of the Bolshevik propaganda commission in New York! And how did they get from Manhattan to Mexico City? ("It may be that they had proper conveyance," she wrote Lieutenant Commander Starr in Norfolk on June 10th. "However, I did not know that this class of people were allowed unlimited privileges in our country; I was under the impression that they were greatly restricted in their travels, especially in those for the purpose of grouping together.")

Just as Miss Bauer does, I wonder too. Maybe she has some undisclosed evidence.

Of course I know nothing of her or of her type of mind, but at least it seems that her plea for investigation should be considered. There may be more back of the Bolshevist idea than we would at first have supposed.

I must write Mr. Richey.

Right now.

W. O. SAUNDERS

Offices of the Independent
505 East Fearing Street
Elizabeth City, North Carolina
June 21, 1921

Hunt on for Pirates—Government Is Seeking Possible Submarine Freebooter, the *Post*'s headlines blared, just warming up. 3 Steamers Vanish in Fairest Weather; Crew Gone from Schooner; Theories Advanced That German U-Boat Captain Is Still Carrying On War, or That Bolsheviks Are Stealing Supplies—Daughter of Missing Captain Forces Action, Base May Be an African Port.

Boy, you read a stack of headlines like *that*, in the *Washington Post* no less, and you knew things were rolling now! According to the *Post*, the federal government was in the sway of two possible theories in connection with "the mysterious pirate ship." Not even "a possible" in there to modify this as-yet-unseen raider. Now she's a *fact*, this ship!

One theory, they say, is that it is being operated by the Soviet government of Russia to obtain supplies which it can not purchase.

And the other theory is that the pirate is a German submarine, commanded by a sea raider who has refused to acknowledge the war as being over, and who is still maintaining himself in some hidden base God knows where.

This, says the *Post*, "is the one held by the Rev. Mr. Lorimer and Miss Wormell, who also advance the theory that the logical base for the vessel would be somewhere on the coast of Africa. Officials frankly say that this theory is as good as any other."

The coast of Africa, can you fathom that?

Well, we've got a whole big batch of Coast Guardsmen coming to town here next week, the big surfmen's get-together, and you can bet I'll look forward to trying a few of these lines of thought out on *them*. These old boys are not what you'd call word-mincers, not a one of them. They're plain-spoken fellows, and I expect they've all got a thought or two on the subject, and, if the *Independent* man here gets his wish and his way, I reckon I'll hear every word of it.

A NOTION FROM NEW ROCHELLE

Home of Clarence Snider
New Rochelle, New York
June 21, 1921

By telephone this evening, Clarence A. Snider, secretary of the Union Sulphur Company, told the *New York Times* he disagreed with the government's notion that his firm's steamer, the 2,294-ton *Hewitt*, was still "afloat and intact." She had sailed from Sabine, Texas, with a load of sulfur for Boston and Portland on January 20 or 21, 1921, and was last heard from—vessel to vessel—about two hundred fifty miles north of Jupiter Inlet, Florida. Union Sulphur posted her as overdue in early February, as missing on March 16.

"No," Snider said, "I don't believe the *Hewitt* is still afloat—we would've heard of it long before this. Anyway, we have collected the insurance on the craft."

W. O. SAUNDERS

Offices of the Independent
505 East Fearing Street
Elizabeth City, North Carolina
June 22, 1921

Well, what about the *Hewitt*? I say.

There are at least *three* mystery ships in this case, and the *Hewitt*'s the second one. Coming up from the south behind the *Deering*, she might've gone down in that big blow January 26th through 28th, she sure might've.

Some seem to think the steamer that came in on the Lookout Light Vessel *was* the *Hewitt*, but that doesn't make any sense at all—*that* ship—she's the third in my mysterious trio—appeared out of the *north* and was southbound, then acted strangely, all that business about refusing the hail from the lightship, and covering its name and changing course to the east.

So what about the *Hewitt*? There was no evidence on the *Deering*'s hull, apparently, that the *Hewitt* or any other vessel collided with the *Deering*, so I'd rule that particularity out. But was the *Hewitt* that "flash of light" folks say they saw off the New Jersey coast the day after the *Deering* ran aground on Diamond Shoals? Had she in fact picked up the *Deering*'s crew off the Carolina coast only to lose them along with her own in that explosion?

I've got to wonder about this . . . we all do.

AN APPEAL FROM THE OLD COUNTRY

From a little corner of England, a small crossroads just a few miles north of Brighton on the south coast, came a letter to Washington, the plea of a pair of frightened parents:

June 1921
To the Bureau of Navigation, Department of Commerce:
    We are very anxious to learn if our son sailed on her [the *Deering*], as he has been missing since the end of January.
    C. And S. Cutler
    Parents of 18-year-old sailor William N. Cutler
    Haywards Heath, Sussex, England

How many must there be, lost boys, run-off-to-sea boys, fought-in-the-War-and-never-returned boys, no-way-to-reach-them-in-the-Great-North-Woods boys, and for every one of them, a woman and a man by a hearth somewhere, graying away and lamenting Lord knows what and praying over this where-in-the-worldness that has overtaken their home, leaving those two intimates with little, or nothing, left to say to each other except an occasional word like *maybe* and, more frequently, tears that whether stifled or unchecked said it all?

We are very anxious to learn . . .

Missing since . . .

LULA WORMELL

Home of Mrs. DeWitt Masterson
822 Potomac Avenue
Buffalo, New York
June 22, 1921

You're from the *Times*, are you not? Yes? Yes, then, I will give you a statement.

"I am positive that Father and the other men of the *Deering* are captives of a pirate band which took possession of the ship, possibly with aid from part of the crew. In fact, we suspect all was not well with at least one of the men shipped on the *Deering*, and this information has been given the authorities in Washington. No one was aboard the *Deering* when it drifted ashore at Hatteras. Full sail was set and the ship's cargo was untouched. The latter is a point that is difficult for me to explain. However, I have gone over all the ground with the government investigators and I hope that something material will soon be brought to light."

Now I have a train to catch for Lowell, Massachusetts, where I will follow up on another clue and then take the Boston and Maine on home.

And, please, you go right on and print what I said—every word of it—in the *New York Times*.

DRUMBEAT

Washington, D.C.

June 22, 1921

Comb Seas for Ships; State Department Pirate Alarm; Starts World-Wide Search; Many Vessels Disappear.

Secretary Hoover met the press on Monday of the fourth week in June, indicating that several ships other than the *Carroll A. Deering* may also have encountered the pirate and his oil-burning crew and letting it be known that the Department of Commerce had prodded Secretary of State Charles Evans Hughes and his department into setting up an international hue and cry. Among these possible casualties was the *Albyn*, a four-masted vessel said to be a Russian bark operating independently of the Soviet government and still flying the flag of old Russia. The *Albyn*, in fact a Finnish ship from Nystad, left Norfolk for Gothenburg, Sweden, October 1, 1920, and was never heard from again.

Then the *Yute*, a Spanish steamer of nearly three thousand tons, sailed from Baltimore November 14, 1920, radioed for help on November 17 from two hundred forty miles southeast of Cape May, and that was the last word from, or of, her.

Among the larger ships now believed to have dropped out of sight, during the period when the State Department and other government officials were inclined to believe that piracy was at its height, was the *Ottawa*, a British tanker with a crew of thirty-three that sailed from Norfolk for Manchester, England, on February 2, 1921, and had her last radio contact with the *Dorington Court* on February 6. When the *Dorington Court*—which had left Hampton Roads the same day as the *Ottawa*—made Le Havre February 21, she reported damage to her superstructure and two boats smashed by very heavy weather on the sea.

The *Ottawa*, meanwhile, had vanished.

The Italian steamship *Monte San Michele* sailed from New York for Genoa on February 2 and last gave her radio position when requesting aid on February 8. Where, pray tell, was she? Or the *Gymeric*; or the

Cabedello, a Brazilian merchantman; or the steamship *Esperanza de La-rrinaga*; the cargo ships *Florino* of Italy and *Svartskog* of Norway; the *Tenzan Maru* of Japan; the *Entine Florina*; the *H. E. Pierce*?

The papers called it "the mystery of the vanished fleet." Ethel Browning, the United Press correspondent, reported that Coast Guard vessels were moving in and out of the inlets of North Carolina's Outer Banks, searching for wreckage and for clues, and that the Department of Commerce might also ask the army and navy for airplanes to fly over the remote barrier beaches near Cape Hatteras. Of the case of the *Deering*, one official invoked Coleridge's *Ancient Mariner* when he remarked, "We might as well have searched a painted ship upon a painted ocean for sight of the vanished crew."

In this climate of confusion and extreme curiosity, the State Department made official its recognition of all these mysterious circumstances and made public what information it had on the schooner *Carroll A. Deering*, and the press picked right up on State's assertion of the *Deering*'s having been found "in such a condition that there was every suspicion of foul play having occurred." Other government departments were proceeding upon the same theory—foul play.

All but the U.S. Navy, which did not in the least partake of all this general excitement over piracy, with Secretary Denby saying he had no report of pirates operating off the American coast—nor did naval officers think piracy could be practiced successfully here.

"If there is any," Secretary Denby said with surety, "the Navy promises to make short work of it."

FROM THE ADMIRAL IN PHILLY
Philadelphia Naval Yard
Philadelphia, Pennsylvania
June 22, 1921

Rear Admiral L. M. Nulton, the commander here in Philadelphia, got into the business of public speculation.

"If there is a pirate craft," he said, "she was or is operating with forged ship's papers. It is always necessary when a ship enters a port to have her papers examined, and this craft could operate for a short time with forged papers, but in the end she would disclose her identity.

"It is true that by stripping vessels of provisions and fuel the outlaw could continue operations a long time, but eventually she would have to put into some port for repairs. Machinery, you know, can not run forever without being overhauled and repaired. If such a craft is operating she will have to return to port at some time, and when she does there will be interesting developments."

N.Y. POLICE RAIDED REDS IN '19, IN '20

New York had been in a fearful thrall of possible violent overthrow all during 1919 and beyond, the leading Red-hunter being a state senator named Clayton R. Lusk, chair of a committee on Bolshevism.

"Any man who says the country is not in danger is uninformed, unintelligent, or disloyal," Senator Lusk proclaimed.

He revealed a Finnish plot against the American government at the very end of 1919, and the very next month—on January 16, 1920—his Joint Legislative Committee Investigating Seditious Activities unveiled a color-coded map of Manhattan and the South Bronx showing "location and extent of Racial Colonies," sections of the city where ethnic communities friendly or potentially receptive to unrest and revolution lay, east side, west side, all around the town. Russians were *red*, Finns and other Scandinavians *mustard yellow*, French and Irish were *black*.

On the 22nd of June 1921, the Associated Press moved a story from New York City, reporting that the New York police now linked the disappearance at sea of several American ships within the last few months with plans revealed to them during a series of raids on radical headquarters a year and a half ago, schemes for the seizure of these vessels at sea and their diversion to Russian Soviet ports. The headlines were unequivocal:

Link Red Pirate Plots with Vanishing of Ships.

Police claimed they were informed "through certain confidential sources" that officials of the Union of Russian Workers of the United

States and Canada—an organization since busted—had encouraged its out-of-work members who knew the sea "to seek employment on American ships, overpower the other members of the crew and direct the vessels to Russia."

Russian anarchists, said the New York police, had used the labor union movement as a camouflage, sparking the authorities to raid their headquarters repeatedly during 1919 and 1920 and to make numerous arrests. Most of those collared in these raids were deported to Russia by way of Finland aboard the U.S. Army transport *Buford*, a ship nicknamed "the Soviet Ark."

Meanwhile, the wire service had it, a worldwide search was on for the so-called mysterious silent ship that disregarded the serious distress call sent out by the Lookout Shoals lightship and that passed near the *Carroll A. Deering* off the North Carolina coast. "The silent ship," said the AP, "is now sought by government bureaus, as a clew of possible value in clearing up the mysterious disappearance of the cargo steamers along the coast off Cape Hatteras. Marine records all over the world are to be examined and ship logs will be compared by experts."

A PANIC IN PARIS

The Eiffel Tower
Paris, France
June 22, 1921

Were it not for the Eiffel Tower's antenna and its wireless, Parisians would have torn it down twelve years earlier as an eyesore whose celebratory concession had run out, as an impediment to the flight of birds. Now and for some time the great soaring mesh of steel had served as the center for the Telegraphie Service Français, the TSF. The German pilot von Decken, from his aircraft, threw a pair of bombs at the tower's wireless station late in September 1914, trying but failing to knock it out, and a year later the first human voice ever to cross the Atlantic sailed in speech from the U.S. Naval Station, Arlington, Virginia, to the tower in Paris. Marconi, the man who invented the wireless to begin with, tuned in from his apartment in Rome and listened to Marshal Foch announcing the armistice that ended the Great War in a marconigram from the Eiffel Tower.

Now poets sang of it, Apollinaire in *Lettre-Océan* centering his "song of the cablegram" around the words "300 meters high"; and the Chilean Huidobro, in *Eiffel Tower*, rhapsodized:

Your wireless telegraphy
Draws words to you
As a rose-arbour draws bees

and called its invisible messaging "the wind from Europe / the electric wind."

The wind on the 22d of June, though, blew in from a different direction, a westerly from Washington, a cabled suggestion from the Americans that European international police join in the hunt for missing ships. The Eiffel Tower's wireless station found itself nearly clogged with a record amount of business, as did other French stations at Bordeaux and Lyon.

Had no one noticed the disappearance of such a large number of ships in the past year and the loss of all the crews without a clue? The news reaching France caused an enormous sensation, and the shipping and marine insurance markets were thrown into a panic, the air of radiotelegraphy and telephony thickening with messages from owners and agents to their vessels out upon the high seas, telling all to be on guard against the mysterious raider.

All Paris quickly believed that one lone madman with a submarine was the pirate wreaking havoc across the hemisphere. But who was he, and where would he strike next? And would *affaires marine* be now as they were in the war just past, with the great shippers of Europe demanding armed protection from the allied navies, which would somehow be expected not only to provide convoy escort, but also to fan out and scour the waters of the world in search of this pariah?

SENT IN FROM SEATTLE

Terminal Station
Seattle, Washington
June 23, 1921
Postmarked 6:30 P.M.

Mr. Herbert Hoover,
Secretary of Commerce

Dear Sir:

Ships on Atlantic and off Hateras captured by small four masted oil burning auxiliary powered bark carring name "*Pontius*." Vessel sails as legitimate cargo carrier and makes captures by displaying distress signs and then using guns. Crews are manacled and thrown overboard. Vessel is operated by Mexican bandits under one Capt. Armas. Present base is small bay Gulf Mexico. The following may be accounted for:

Schr *Lea*,———sunk
Str *Hewitt*,———sunk
Str *Wm.*———, *disguised* now Victorious,———Mexico
Deering,———ashore
Yute,———held for sale gulf Mexico
Albin,———sunk
Westerly,———ashore

They will operate again in Sept.

FROM THE COMMISSIONER
OF NAVIGATION HIMSELF

Brooklyn, New York
June 23, 1921

"I have heard many tall yarns of the sea," said E. T. Chamberlain, U.S. Commissioner of Navigation, to the *Brooklyn Times*. He seemed to be on the verge of denigrating the rumors of missing ships and piratical feats.

"But in this case the facts are there. The *Carroll A. Deering* met some strange fate beyond that of ordinary vessels come to grief."

W. O. SAUNDERS

Offices of the Independent
505 East Fearing Street
Elizabeth City, North Carolina
Late June 1921

Now it all made sense, said some here in Betsy Town.

"*What* all you talking about?" said others.

The Reds, the Bolsheviki, the goddamn godless Communists, that's what. (Oh, yes, people spoke that way—they were *that* forthright and profane!) You heard people saying things about the Bolshevists like, "S.O.S., ship or shoot—put them on stone ships with lead sails and let them sail away to hell!"

Sometimes it seemed to me the whole country'd gone crazy about the Reds, Elizabeth City along with all the rest. Well, sure, there were all those mail bombs the other year, to the mayor of Seattle and the senator from Georgia and then somebody at the post office found a whole batch of them that were supposed to go to President Wilson's cabinet and the Supreme Court! And that bomber who walked up onto Attorney General Palmer's porch in Washington and, well, he didn't do much damage to Mr. A. Mitchell Palmer, but he apparently made one hell of a noise blowing his own self up.

And the May Day riots, true—police getting a melee going out in Cleveland on account of somebody was flying a red flag at the front of a Socialist parade and wouldn't take it down. Soldiers and sailors busting through a huge crowd in Manhattan and raiding the Socialist newspaper, the *New York Call*, and clubbing seven staffers hard enough to send them to the hospital.

Now, for an editor like myself, that last item's hitting a little too close to home!

But, on the other hand, none of that happened *here*. Though to hear some folks talk, you'd think our shipyards and potato fields were just full of Bolsheviks, ready to jump up and take over. Well, all right, then, *bring* me one! I'll shine a light on him and interview him and expose the whole plot, if there is one.

Can't do it, can you?

No. But you can't keep people from talking, either. Never could, never will. Why God made us, I reckon.

The New York papers I read told about a bunch of raids the police made just last year, about how the Soviet sailors were plotting to sign articles and get onto American ships with American masters, to worm their way into the confidences of their unwitting mates, to rise up with them in mutiny, and then sail away back to Mother Russia.

Sounds incredible, I know, but I am telling you this Red scare was real—and it's not over, not by a country mile.

Now here's another item from up in Manhattan—New York's finest proved too fine for what Communists they did turn up, the New York Police Department bomb squad in particular. Detective Sergeant James J. Gegan got them, caught the ringleaders in a raid on the headquarters of the United Russian Workers of the United States and Canada, down at 133 East Fifteenth Street. There was a big meeting going on, and Gegan's squad rounded up three hundred men and women. Sergeant Gegan and his men questioned the Russians, and before any of them were deported, learned of secret sessions of the Russian Workers where all these mutinies were plotted.

At about the time of the East Fifteenth Street raid, several vessels, according to the papers I read, were having trouble with their crewmen. The freighter *William O'Brien*, missing since April 1920, sailed for Rotterdam but put back into the Port of New York only a day later, and the ship's master reported "trouble with the crew" as the reason for her return. After one day in port during which the captain replaced his chief engineer, the *O'Brien* made another try, and three days later the steamship *Baltic* picked up a mayday from her saying she was five hundred miles off Cape May, needing help. From this second sailing she neither returned nor made port, ever, anywhere else.

"In view of yesterday's disclosures," said the front page of the *New*

York Times, "the possibilities of this craft having fallen into the hands of Bolshevist adherents was discussed with much concern."

So, you see, that was what all made sense about the *Carroll A. Deering* to some. I'm not saying I believe all that from the police, or that this is what happened to the *Deering*, now—I'm just laying it out, the kind of thing people're reading and hearing about and talking up and have been all along, all spring while this Ghost Ship story's been unfolding. So now we've got fisher folk out on the coast of Carolina here thinking there're crews of piratical Russians hovering out at sea, just over the horizon, waiting to seize whomever or whatever happens by.

And, lest we forget, there was the so-called mad German, the rogue submariner still fighting the Great War two years and more after the armistice. What about him, folks said, and not the Russians at all?

And there was a third notion put forth, one of predacious sailors loyal to no land, no law, and no one but their own sorry selves, a modern-day Brethren of the Coast, maybe even the crowd who by some accounts had made off with the U.S. Navy's collier *Cyclops* three years ago and lain up with their stolen craft in some Amazon River hideout till whenever they had need to prowl the seas again.

So read the ms. found in a bottle, I say, and then read it again. Now we knew who had made off with the *Deering*'s crew that dark night on the Outer Banks. It was those Bolshevik Russian sailors. It was the rogue German. It was the pirates of the collier *Cyclops*.

Now it all made sense. Or did it?

TOPICS OF THE TIMES
Times Square
New York, New York
June 23, 1921

"Piracy is a remote possibility," concluded the *New York Times* in its lead editorial of the day, commenting in the main on the veracity and, indeed, sensibility of the note fisherman Gray found back in April in a bottle washed up at Buxton Beach, North Carolina.

"If the handwriting has been identified conclusively," said the *Times*, "that comes near to proving that the *Deering* and her crew did have some strange and exciting experience. What it was is a dark mystery as yet. Had there been a seizure of the vessel in an old-fashioned mutiny, surely the mate would have said so, or at least given some hint of the fact, unless, indeed, he was himself the leader of the mutiny.

"The theory of pirates cannot pass for more than expressing about the remotest of present-day possibilities, and even that amount of credence demands crediting to the Bolsheviki an amount and kind of enterprise of which their known proceedings have given no hint. . . . It is not easy to imagine a Russian pirate getting safely to and through the Baltic or into the Black Sea. Nowhere else would he have a market. In every port, doubtless, there still are men who would deal in stolen goods and be quite unprejudiced against piracy, but shipping regulations everywhere are against such traffic and make it so difficult and dangerous as to be impracticable. The pirates, nowadays, are all on land, and nobody worse than sneaky smugglers is afloat."

Elsewhere in the *Times*, local shipping men gave the credit for doing in the missing ships to the weather and to floating mines left over from the Great War. How could pirates prey upon so many ships, they mused, without giving themselves away?

HEAVY WEATHER

Washington, D.C.
Friday, June 24, 1921

One of the nation's top weathermen bet upon wintry gales for causing the ruin of so many ships. F. G. Tingley, chief meteorologist for the Weather Bureau's marine division, pointed to records in his office that told of a vast storm extending over a thousand-mile area and affecting virtually all of the North Atlantic shipping lanes.

"Most of the missing vessels sailing late in January and early in February," Tingley told the *Washington Post*, "were caught in the storm area. For three days, from February 6th through 9th, the velocity of the wind was from 75 to 90 miles an hour with the barometer down to 28.8

inches. Again on February 15th a gale developed in mid ocean and raged for three days.

"With regard to the schooner *Carroll A. Deering* reported off Hatteras breaking up with the storm of February 20, Weather Bureau officials believe that her crew attempted to go ashore when the schooner first struck at Cape Hatteras and were lost."

Tingley waved before the *Post*'s reporter a list of twenty ships— ships damaged in various ways by the winter storms, their boats carried off and so forth, but all of which made port—to compare with the Commerce Department's list of twenty missing ships from the Atlantic lanes in early 1921.

"From this list," said Tingley, "it can be seen that we have definite reports of heavy weather in the North Atlantic early in February. The wireless message picked up by the *Buenos Aires* on February 7th may have been from the missing steamer, the *Hewitt*. Storms at sea are not uncommon, but the February storms were the worst in years. As far as I am concerned there is nothing so very mysterious about vessels being lost in storms such as that.

"We are not worried much," Tingley concluded, "about Bolshevik submarines or pirates."

At Lloyd's of London, the top men concurred with Tingley, dismissing the very concept of pirates going after freighters with cargoes that could not easily be converted into cash and comparing the high seas and heavy weather of early 1921 to the terrific gales of 1899, all in all putting down piracy in even pithier fashion than the American weatherman. The last word from Lloyd's was:

"Fantastic."

Yet whether the weatherman was worried or not, the fact was that the *Cabedello*, a Brazilian steamer bound for Oran, Algeria, which turned up some good time later in the French port of Marseilles, was the only ship to make *both* lists.

SENATOR SIMMONS OF NORTH CAROLINA

U.S. Senate
Washington, D.C.
June 1921

Senator Furnifold McLendel Simmons, author of North Carolina's race-baiting campaigns of 1898 and 1900 and leader of the state's
liquor-ban referendum of 1908, also took a proprietary interest in the
state's rivers, harbors, and ports, and he found plenty to intrigue him
in the mystery of the *Carroll A. Deering*.

For one thing, since the *Deering* had just come up from Barbados,
that Carib island awash in rum, the prohibitionist figured there might
be rumrunning involved somehow in the schooner's unusual grounding and the inexplicable disappearance of its crew. For another, Herbert Hoover was out in front on this case, and Simmons liked Hoover
because he was a dry—liked him so much that years later, in 1928, Simmons would endorse Hoover for president in a move that proved to be
Simmons's undoing.

But in mid-1921, the senator from North Carolina—the New Bern
attorney born on his father's plantation up Pollocksville way whom the
down-home folks now called "the top-dog Democrat," the machine
politician with the big broad mustache—would rise to the occasion
and see what he could do to take advantage of the *Deering* disaster and
gain more federal money to fight the modern blockade runners, the
ones he suspected of all odd and foul deeds occurring along the Carolina coast, the swashbucklers with rumbarrels in their holds.

"Are there enough Coast Guard cutters out patrolling our coast?"
Senator Simmons asked the Senate of the United States.

"No, no, and no!" he complained, "there are *not*! Liquor running
is being indulged in *freely* off the North Carolina coast, and a Coast
Guard vessel should be sent down there just to look out for violators of
the Volstead Act."

"A SILLY SEASON SCARE"

Wall Street
New York, New York
Friday, June 24, 1921

The *New York Times* and the panic-stricken Parisians might all entertain the possibility of piracy in the case of the *Carroll A. Deering* and other missing ships, but the *Wall Street Journal* would have none of it.

"Secretaries in a new Administration have a tendency to go off half-cocked," said the *Journal's* editors on the front page, suggesting that the "usually sedate Secretary Hughes" should take a look at "a few unro-mantic books of reference before the United States Navy is called out to chase mythical pirates."

The *Journal* applied an actuarial skepticism to the entire set of pro-ceedings surrounding the missing-ships stories, noting that at least one rival in the press, the *Baltimore Sun*, was padding its list with names of ships from nearly a year back and with others whose disappearances were undated.

"In normal non-submarine years a certain proportion of ships, suf-ficiently constant for calculation by the underwriters, sail and never make port," wrote the *Journal*. "In a few years before the war there are official records of 21 such vessels in 1911, 30 in 1912, 24 in 1913, and 27 in 1914. Nothing was mentioned about 'pirates' in those years. The ves-sels seem to have sunk without trace, without even a waterlogged dere-lict as mute evidence of another mystery of the sea. For the sailorman it is all in the day's work. They that go down to the sea in ships occa-sionally see wonders of which no human record remains.

"There is no need for a warm weather attack of nerves about it. The whole thing is a newspaper sensation, worked up in ignorance of the ship mortality tables. It is a silly-season scare, to which our dependable old friend the sea serpent will probably soon succeed, while the enor-mous gooseberry is ripening in Sullivan County.

"But, incidentally, do the Departments of State and of Commerce possess ordinary books of reference, or, what is more to the point, do they ever consult them?"

TWO CENTS WORTH

San Antonio, Texas
June 24, 1921
Postmarked 10:30 A.M.

George Washington, left profile, canted leftward from a two-cent stamp on the postcard's upper corner, giving the impression the first president was staring slantwise at the address, "Commerce Department, Washington D.C." A postman handstamped the time and date and with a wavy staff of seven lines canceled the postage, never stopping to read—as would his more rural and small-town counterparts—the bitter song on the verso of the card:

TO WHOME IT MAY CONCERNE.

I NOW WRITE TO SAY THAT YOU WILL BE TO THE GOOD IF YOU DO NOT TRY TO SOLVE THE MYSTERY OF THE SHIP DEERING. IT IS THE 1921 MYSTERY AND THE ONLY ONE TO TELL THE TALE IS BOUND IN IRONS AND WILL STAY UNTILL HE DIES. THIS IS ALL FOR REVENGE AND AS WE ALL SAY REVENGENCE IS SWEET.

I AM YOURS

23-23.

SOLVE?

Lawrence Richey's office got this anonymous warning in Washington six days later, at half past high noon.

W. O. SAUNDERS

Offices of the Independent
505 East Fearing Street
Elizabeth City, North Carolina
June 24, 1921

Captain Ralph Temple Crowley, the Coast Guard's new District 7 superintendent here in Elizabeth City, stopped in to talk, and I was mighty glad to see him and hear what he had to say about this mysterious mess.

Let me just tell you a thing or two about him. He's forty-six, hasn't been here in Betsy Town very long—he's only recently arrived in the sound country, and has come to take over District 7 from Edgar Chadwick. Says he's a real Maine Down Easter, a native of Jonesport, near the Great Wass Island Station where he used to be keeper. And wouldn't you know, just before getting the call to Elizabeth City, Captain Crowley served as keeper of the South Portland Station in Maine?

Right where the captain of the schooner *Deering* was from. So of course I asked him about all that, and he proved that when it was called for he could be a man of few words.

"Well," Captain Crowley said, "in the matter of the *Carroll A. Deering*, I have no fear of pirates."

No fear. Now that's the kind of thing you like to hear from the Coast Guard. No fear at all.

SEEN BY THE *LAKE ARLINE*

The Atlantic Ocean
100 miles southeast of Cape Hatteras
June 24, 1921

The master of the American steamship *Lake Arline* spotted what he took to be a phantom craft, with black-painted hull and a lookout platform on each mast, two men stationed upon each one. Thirty men prowled her decks, two large white motorboats hung from davits on the sides, and astern was a white whaleboat and a yellow dory.

The vessel had no name in evidence.

Too deep way out here for fishing, thought the *Lake Arline*'s captain. Light weather and she's hove to, going nowhere and in no hurry—a smuggler?

THEORY OF PIRATES BORNE OUT
Washington, D.C.
June 24, 1921

Seeking to bolster its theory that high-seas pirates were behind the disappearances of over twenty ships in recent months, the Department of State today released a detailed official account of the seizure in April 1920 of the German fishing schooner, the *Senator Schroeder* of Cuxhaven, by a mutinous crew acting in the name and interests of Soviet Russia.

The *Senator Schroeder* sailed from Cuxhaven, a small north German port east of the Frisian Islands, on the 21st of April 1920, bound for Iceland. A short time after sailing, the captain discovered three stowaways aboard and then leniently gave them the liberty of the ship till the next port of call. Miles out at sea, the stowaways—having corrupted the five able-bodied seamen aboard the vessel and gotten them in league—lured the captain into the crew's quarters, overpowered him, then locked him up and threw the first mate, first engineer, and the ship's one passenger in with him. The second mate, second engineer, cook, and two stokers ran the ship for ten days under threat of death, sailing north by order of the mutineers all the way around Scandinavia to the Russian port of Murmansk on the Barents Sea.

Once there, a sailor named Kneufen claimed the *Senator Schroeder* for the Soviet government and moved his prisoners first to a jail in Murmansk, then on the fifth of May to Petrograd. Only after a month were the captain, engineer, and mate allowed to go home to Germany.

The *Senator Schroeder* set sail again to fish, now under command of officers loyal to Kneufen and Soviet Russia. But a second mutiny occurred, this one promulgated by the German crew who had worked the ship all along and who now reclaimed it. After calling at Tromsö, Norway, and Bergen, Germany, the *Senator Schroeder*, under rightful authority, returned to its home port of Cuxhaven, where Kneufen and all the other mutineers were swiftly tried and sentenced for piracy on the high seas, Kneufen getting five years in prison for his acts against ship and crew.

Given the case of the *Senator Schroeder*, was it any wonder that Soviet-stimulated piracy as a theory for the disappearance and disposition of the *Carroll A. Deering* aroused sympathy in the government and among the people of the United States? Why, the *Washington Post*'s man in Vladivostok reported a number of vessels—their names all effaced—coming into that eastern Russian port, all with Russian crews, at a time when at least ten other ships had likewise vanished from the Atlantic shipping lanes. And this was *since* the *William O'Brien*, which perhaps had fallen to a mutinous Bolshevik crew, steamed past the Statue of Liberty and off into nowhere.

Where on earth had the ships of the vanished fleet all sailed away to?

And where was the American steamer *Hewitt*, with her crew of forty, the ship that was apparently so close in following the *Carroll A. Deering* north past Lookout Shoals Light Ship?

RED ROVERS
Portland, Maine
June 24, 1921

"Delightfully dramatic is the mental vision of the Bolsheviks as Red Rovers on the high seas," commented the *Portland Evening Express and Daily Advertiser*. Even this journal, highly interested in the current maritime crisis as hometown paper of both the *Deering*'s captain and the *Hewitt*'s crew, found the alarm sounded by Hoover and Hughes as questionable as did the *Wall Street Journal*, continuing:

"Doubtless Trotzky, if he had a living chance, could give points to the late Captain Kidd, or the late Sir Henry Morgan, and discount them at their own game. He has the face and presence for such a role. . . . Yet Lenin is subject to sea-sickness and Trotzky has other fish to fry—not deep-sea fish. And what Russia could do with a merchant marine if one were presented to her gratis, it would take a Philadelphia lawyer to find out."

BELIEVES PIRATES TOOK OVER CREW
Buffalo, New York
June 25, 1921

No matter what Chief R. T. Crowley thought and sounded off about down in Elizabeth City, the previous 7th District Coast Guard chief begged to differ.

"It is quite probable that a pirate ship is on the Atlantic and that this ship took the crew of the schooner *Deering* to help man her," said Superintendent Edgar Chadwick, U.S. Coast Guard, to the *Washington Post*. Superintendent Chadwick, who served the Atlantic Coast district for years and "knew every inch of the coast from Maine to Florida and most of the ocean inside the 3-mile limit," according to the *Post*, was in Buffalo on an inspection tour of stations on the Great Lakes.

"It does not seem possible that a ship could have been in distress without the numerous life-saving stations down there hearing or knowing something about it," Chadwick said. "It looks very certain that a pirate crew boarded the *Deering* at sea and commanded the crew to transfer to the outlaw ship. The case would tend to show that the pirate ship was short of hands and held up the first boat in sight, which happened to be the *Deering*."

Chadwick based his theory on the fact that the *Deering* carried no cargo of value to a raider, and that when she brought up on the shoals there was nothing wrong with her. As many vessels as had turned up missing lately, mused Chadwick, there must be one awfully desperate ship out there sailing the seas.

W. O. SAUNDERS

Offices of the Independent
505 East Fearing Street
Elizabeth City, North Carolina
June 28–30, 1921

Well, a couple weeks back we had a big to-do with Teddy Roosevelt's son, Colonel Theodore Roosevelt who's now the assistant navy
secretary, in town to approve the gear for the surfmen's meeting and
big marine show on the Pasquotank River, two naval hydroplanes, all
the surf apparatus. Couple of hometowners were back with us:
Colonel Ike Meekins—he's counsel to the Alien Property Custodian up
in Washington—and Hallett Ward, our congressman, he was here, too.

Just to check out the gear for the show!

Then this week into town the surfmen came, not just the boys from
the Outer Banks, who are always sailing up here on leave, but the
whole Surfman's Benevolent Association from all over the east coast.
They were here to have a big time, just as they'd had in 1919, the last
time Betsy Town was their meeting place. If any of them are disappointed by our little town on the Narrows, you couldn't prove it by me
or anybody else in Betsy!

Course, Elizabeth City *was* where the Surfmen's Association got its
start about twenty years back. Before '19, they were here in '13 and *that*
was a hot time in the old town—five thousand people showed up for
the marine sports, I kid you not! Now, that's a passel of folks, especially
when you realize there are only about 2,800 in the whole Coast Guard
itself, and a little over eight hundred in the surfmen's group.

They put on quite a display back then, and they were here to show
off this time, too!

Really, it was a thrilling exhibition of the newest and latest Coast
Guard lifesaving apparatus in actual use. The navy got in on it, too,
running hydroplane races, big roostertail wakes geysering up into the
sky over the Pasquotank. Let me tell you, a power surfboat in a blackwater river like the Pasquotank here is some kind of sight, and in one

race between a hydroplane and a superpowered motor boat, we clocked them both making forty-five miles an hour!

Then to settle everybody down, they had a tub race, too, with the contestants paddling by hand. You should've seen them, pulling their stunts in the river down at the foot of Main Street, the cameramen from Fox and Pathé shooting film of it all.

They even caught the duck race with those cameras, where twenty ducks were released midstream and a dozen swimmers tried to catch them, and one of them was Captain Bannister Midgett, the champion swimmer of the Outer Banks, there to take on all comers and he was sixty-seven years young! Then the canoe-tilting contest. Hot, I mean! Thousands of people lining the shore, tanks of ice-water along our streets, scores of canoes and motorboats and small craft out on the water.

The surfboat race, now, that was the big deal, came up about four o'clock. They ran upriver, starting from Elizabeth City Iron Works on the south side of the river, and when they pulled even with Main Street they capsized their boats just to show what they could do—all hands thrown into the water, the men instantly re-righting their boats. These boys are what you call *good*! First one to the drawbridge with all crew and gear won, and when it was all over but the whole town and county shouting, John Allen Midgett's crew came out ahead by half a boat length.

Captain Midgett wasn't so lucky, though, in the schooner rescue contest. The deal here was this: the surfmen were timed, starting with the firing of the Lyle gun and the shot-line's going out to the schooner (they had the *John S. Wilson* tied up in the river), and Crew 2, from Whalehead Station, came back with the winning time of eight minutes.

That was Tuesday.

Then they got back out there on the river Wednesday morning and did it all over *again* for the cameras, for close-ups and all.

A Coast Guard airplane came straight on in, directly I mean *at* that schooner, flying so low across its bow you'd've thought something was going to go, the bowsprit or the jibstays or the airplane's landing gear, *something*! That was quite a thing to behold, I'm telling you, and it was sure enough some nervy flying. And the fellows in the plane dropped the lifeline so close to the schooner the camera caught the splash of the line in the water—now, can you beat that?

I have to put in a good word, too, about the cameramen, because another time the surfmen fired a lifeline from the mortar on shore out to the disabled ship. The cannon they shot the line from flipped in the recoil—that's right, did a somersault! Those fellows with the camera shooting it all close-up, they held their ground, didn't bat an eye and got their picture.

More thrills in the restaging Wednesday than in the actual show on Tuesday, I'd warrant. And the whole show wasn't out on the Pasquotank River, either. They had Ziegler's fifteen-piece band playing. Had Hertford set to play Edenton in baseball Wednesday evening, and these were semi-pros, now, and that game was hot as the weather, I tell you: Edenton at bat, down 6–2, top of the ninth inning, but the Hertford pitcher was tired and Edenton hit him for five runs and put Hertford into the bottom of the ninth down 7–6! Two men on, two outs, and Hertford popped out with an infield fly and Edenton carried the day! Whale of a game, and nobody went home disappointed.

All the games and contests aside, there were a lot of nice words and a real good feeling at the banquet Tuesday night down at the Southern Hotel, the big oxblood brick building here at the corner of Main and Road. We ate roast chicken and winekream and homemade chocolate cake, and, for afterward, the drugstores had donated cigars and cigarettes for the men.

The crowd gave Captain John Allen Midgett a huge ovation—that was for leading the rescue of all those British sailors when the *Mirlo* was mined back in the war. A quartet of Negro singers sang old plantation songs and then clog-danced for the guests. Ralph Pool read a poem he'd written, called "Our Life Savers," that ended with the couplet:

We'll rejoice in their coming, meet them, greet them here and try
In some measure now to thank them that they dare to serve—and
die.

Then Captain Bannister Midgett sent forward a motion for a special rising vote of thanks to the Young Women's Club for putting together such a fine banquet and making the surfmen all so welcome here in Betsy. And Chief of Operations Oliver Maxam leapt to his feet and said, "In behalf of the home office at Washington and in behalf of the Coast Guard service from Waddy Head to Brazos, from Brazos to the Golden Gate, and from the Golden Gate to Flattery Island, I second that motion!"

After the sliding of chairs and the men's all standing in place and applauding loudly and at length, the roar of approval from townsmen and surfmen alike, Chief Maxam went on: "You men who stand guardian over the beaches, you men who have made history on these coasts, oft times at terrible sacrifice, the story of which has never been told . . . I salute you one and all!"

Again came a great roar and handclapping and table slapping, noises as joyful as they were serious and sincere, for taken all together, they said "Yes, this is who we are and why we are and this is all about what we do," and I thought, My God, there really are times in this life when we may find ourselves as people not in conflict but bonded together for common purpose and common good, when we can know and acknowledge the very best in ourselves and the very best we can do for each other and this above all was one of those times, and I swear I felt as moved in the Southern Hotel banquet hall that evening in the absolute middle of all those uniformed surfmen and ladies in their finery as I ever have at any time during my brief moment on this earth.

When they were all done, they made a unanimous decision to come back to Elizabeth City same time next year—mind you, unanimous! And these boys have been around, held their shindigs all over—Boston, Providence, Atlanta, Norfolk, Ocean City, even *Coney Island*. But I say, nowhere do they have the good time that they have at Elizabeth City.

Even I managed to get up and say a few words, and I'm glad I did, too.

Because, you know, when you get to thinking about all the mishaps lately out on the Banks, it's easy to see what a need we have for these fellows. And at no time like the present. Shipwrecks know no season,

Surfmen, Cape Hatteras Coast Guard Station No. 183, summer 1921

really—but if they did, I'd say last winter and spring would've been a doozy, what with the *Deering* in January and then first of June the schooner *Laura A. Barnes*, her hold full of sugar, left high and dry on Bodie Island, people driving out to look it over in their balloon-tire Model-T Fords.

And it wasn't even two weeks before the *Laura Barnes* came in that we lost another schooner, the *Mary J. Haynie*, sunk in Pamlico Sound five miles in from Ocracoke Inlet. That's a boat had already been sunk once, they tell me, in the ocean just off Portsmouth Island back in aught-eight. Cutter *Pamlico* refloated her then, but she'll float no more after this. Total loss, her and all her cargo, seven thousand dollars worth of uninsured pianos and organs and other musical instruments that the Duff Piano Company here in Betsy was sending down thataway. When I spoke to Mr. Duff, the owner, you know what he told me? He just shook his head and showed his stoical side and said,

"We may now say that we have furnished music to everything in eastern North Carolina, including the wild, wild waves."

Some of the Coast Guard brass came down from Washington, sure did. W. E. Reynolds, the commandant himself, was in town, mixing free and easy as you please with the men, and seeming genuinely interested in the well-being of the men and the corps. And you could tell by Chief Maxam's jocularity that not only was he enjoying himself immensely, but also that he, too, was certainly no stranger to the surfmen.

Our chamber of commerce liked to have knocked itself out over this event—why, the chamber gave our visitors tickets redeemable for cigars and cold drinks and ice cream at any drugstore in town, and admission to the movies at the Alkrama Theater. And they weren't about to stop there—any surfman who wanted one could get in on an automobile ride down the brick road to Weeksville, where awaiting them at the end of the road was a barrel of lemonade and more boxes of cigars!

Some of them, of course, were looking for whiskey, and Betsy never stood in anybody's way there, not for long. You could find a blind tiger down in the Second Ward, down there near the river, no problem. Everybody talked against it, preached against it, stayed riled up about it—but we were a whiskey town and we all knew it. First town of any size you'd hit if you were, say, a bootlegger with a boat, bringing white liquor up across Albemarle Sound from where they made it down in the East Lake swamps on your way to Norfolk, that navytown queen where you knew you could sell anything so long as it had sin written all over it, although, as the man in Manteo says, when they get around to writing the book of sin, Elizabeth City's going to need its own chapter. Yes, you'd hit Betsy first, and some of it—a *goodly* sum of it—always gets siphoned off for local use. So here we were, looking the other way and hoping the East Lake boys hadn't tossed too many dead cats or automobile batteries into the mash to speed up the distilling process. I tell you, the things some people will drink—anything that'll burn, it seems!

We still haven't gotten over Easter around here yet. All the preachers and churches have been carrying on for months about *the dance evil*, and don't you know these folks at the Easter Dance played right into their hands—drinking, spooning, immoral practices generally. Why, one woman was seen hanging out of the third-floor window of the Robinson building, where the Masonic Hall was, throwing up. And another woman—a *married* woman—apparently got so intoxicated that she kept on dancing after the music had stopped and, when she was so informed, exclaimed to her male companion, "What the hell do you care if the music's stopped, so long as you have me in your arms?"

The Masons canceled any further dances in their hall, and said at this rate they would set Freemasonry back a century before the year was out.

But most of these fellows from the Coast Guard, now, they were decent boys and they weren't here to get all liquored up and fall in the gutter. They were most all of them a credit to their uniforms and we liked that. We were a right patriotic town, in the best sense of it (when we weren't all in a lather over the Bolsheviks), with the Great War just over and all. We were proud to be that way, too, and I know it showed. Couple months back, in late April, we had just buried or, I should say, *re*buried the only Pasquotank County soldier killed in the war, and that really was a day to remember.

He was Corporal Seth Perry, a boy from Okisko on the way to Hertford, who fell crossing a field of fire in Bellecourt, France, trying to warn an American company that was pinned down and couldn't see Germans advancing on them that a surprise attack was about to happen. Though he didn't get the message through, he gave his all, trying. He was in Company K of the 119th Infantry, and he'd volunteered, too, for that last run of his. Blackjack Pershing gave him a citation, sent Seth's mother his Distinguished Service Cross.

The day of the reinterment, there were thousands of people downtown on the courthouse lawn to see him buried there in his flag-draped casket, flowers all over it, and to see it lowered into a grave right here in the midst of us.

Fifty little girls marched single file past his grave and, as they did, each in turn dropped a flower into it.

A bugler played taps.

The Episcopal choir sang "America" and "Onward, Christian Soldiers."

Seth Perry's mother couldn't be there, but his sister could, and it was to her that Jerome Flora, the American Legion's post commander, gave the folded flag from her brother's coffin. She told those around her, loud enough for quite a few to hear, that she had wanted him, her closest kin, back home, not in some foreign field but back here in Betsy Town among friends and family.

Above all, she said, you wanted to know where your people were buried and where they were going to spend eternity. It still hurt—hurt something terrible even though he'd been dead going on three years now, but, such a day, to see how many folks came out and saluted him, a hero. Does your heart good, she said, to see all of you, and to know where he is at last.

Better to know, she kept saying, it's just so much better to know.

GUMSHOE IN DARE COUNTY (1)
Hatteras Island, North Carolina
June 24–July 7, 1921

Agent Thompson came down from the FBI's Raleigh office to the Carolina coast to visit all the Coast Guard stations on Hatteras Island and see what he might turn up in the strange case of the *Carroll A. Deering*.

One of the first things he heard was that not everyone considered it so strange.

At Chicamacomico Station No. 179, twenty-five miles north of Outer Diamond Shoals, Captain John Allen Midgett and his men told Agent Thompson that no wreckage or bodies from the *Mirlo*—mined, burned, and sunk just five miles off this point—had ever washed ashore here or at any point along the coast. They all thought piracy was a fanciful absurdity, and, as Captain Midgett credited offshore currents with carrying all traces of the *Mirlo* and her men on out to sea and to the ocean's deep, he more than implied that the same flows may well have carried the *Deering*'s men in the ship's boats far, far from shore, to their end.

Captain Hooper of Big Kinnakeet Station No. 182, just seven miles above the Outer Diamond, had led his whole crew down to assist then-keeper B. B. Miller of the cape station on the morning of January 31. He and his men had had more time than most to think about the *Deering*, and more firsthand observation of her, too.

"I've been in the Coast Guard thirty-one years," Captain Hooper said, "and never known a vessel to last over three days on the shoals. The *Deering* made it for several weeks, swinging around with the wind just like a weathervane."

"What do you think," asked Agent Thompson, "about the idea of the *Deering's* crewmen abandoning the schooner somewhere after she'd gotten out of sight of the Lookout lightship and before she struck the shoals—and coming ashore in the ship's boats?"

Big Kinnakeet's keeper and crew all shook their heads no.

"Impossible," said Captain Hooper. "From Cape Hatteras to Cape Lookout, the coast is too well patrolled at night, and a lookout maintained all day, for anyone to land a boat at any place along the coast at anytime day or night, without attracting attention."

What the Kinnakeeters all found suspicious about the entire incident was the story they'd gotten that the *Deering* had been plundered *before* the salvors from Hatteras Village got to her on Valentine's Day.

Captain B. R. Ballance at Cape Hatteras station, who had taken over for Captain Miller upon Miller's retirement the very week of the *Deering* disaster, thought it would have been suicide to attempt to launch the ship's boats after she struck, and even if the captain and crew had successfully done so, they wouldn't have been able to carry off all manner of clothing and gear, and they *certainly* couldn't have stopped to round up the davits from which the ship's boats normally hung, as if the boats were still hanging.

"I believe they abandoned her after taking everything of value," said Captain Ballance, "and ran her up on the shoals intentionally—why, all the sails were set full on the port side! If they'd grounded accidentally, no crew would've left the sails set full—they'd've hauled em down and tried to get clear of the shoals!"

Beside the Cape Hatteras Coast Guard Station, the navy now had a

Radio Compass Station of its own, and operator W. H. Gallihan came forth to speak with Agent Thompson. Gallihan, it so happened, had been the radioman on Captain Jacobson's Lookout light vessel that Saturday afternoon in January when the *Carroll A. Deering* passed by and hailed them.

"There was a large number of men all over the decks and no signs of an officer aboard," Gallihan said. "They were the hardest looking bunch of men I've ever seen, and all of them in old clothes. Appeared to me to be foreigners, but I sure don't know what nation they claimed, or what nation would claim them. Then that foreign steamer came by and wouldn't answer any of our signals—oh, we started for her, because my wireless was out, to try and get her to take a radio message and report the *Deering*'s having lost her anchors. Soon as she saw us start, she put on more steam and ran away. Seemed to be following the *Deering*."

Agent Thompson now found his way to the very source of the piracy stories, to the fisherman who had back in April discovered the alarming note in a washed-up bottle, Christopher Columbus Gray, whose house was in Buxton nearby. Gray's tale was a simple one: he had been out hauling driftwood up from the beach at Hatteras Cove, and he spotted the bottle on a pile of drift at a point along the beach about three miles west of the Cape Hatteras Coast Guard Station.

"It looked like it'd just washed up," Gray told the agent. "A pint bottle, clear glass—I could see the note through the bottle. The message was written in ink and on a half sheet of paper. The stopper wasn't sealed and the paper was wet when I took it from the bottle—I was able to get it out with a stick."

Being a detective, Thompson naturally inquired up and down the coast during his purposeful ramble of Hatteras Island as to Gray's reputation and character.

"It was found," the agent noted, "to be of the best."

Intentional, Agent Thompson kept hearing. Over and over again he got the line about someone or ones intentionally running the ship up onto the shoals, stripping and abandoning her. Yet, one Coast Guardsman told him, for the *Deering* to have hit the Outer Diamond in the position she had when they arrived, she would have had to be abandoned within three miles of the shoals—and to the westward—to have hit them with no one aboard. Julian Styron, keeper of Station No. 186 at Hatteras Inlet, stated that the grounding was intentional for sure, and then added fat to that fire:

"At the point on Outer Diamond Shoals where the *Deering* was stranded the bank of the shoals is straight up and down—it would be possible for anyone knowing the water to run a vessel within a hundred feet of where the *Deering* lay and experience no danger either to themselves or the vessel. This grounding was done by someone who knew the water and the shoals."

But who? And why? And for what possible gain? Agent Thompson was left to wonder, noting the Outer Banks consensus in his report of July 8: "Practically everyone along the coast regards the condition of the *Deering* as evidence of a mutiny or forcible taking. . . . Further investigation will be made."

THE *MUNALBRO* IS APPROACHED
Off Long Island, New York
Latitude 39°55'N
Longitude 70°55'W
June 30, 1921
1:45 A.M.

After a day and night of fog the mists lifted, and Captain Elisha Diamond, second officer of the Munson Steamship Line's SS *Munalbro*, bound from Boston to Baltimore, spied the masthead and range lights—but no sidelights—of a westbound steamer, pegging it at "about two points forward of our port beam."

The dark steamer came in making nearly twenty knots, then stopped about a half a mile from the *Munalbro* and killed her engines. "She appeared to be sizing us up," said Diamond. After a quarter-hour she reversed course and then cruised eastward, straight out to sea, and she was out of the officer's sight in a mere two minutes.

Captain Giles of the *Munalbro* filed this report with Munson's Baltimore office, which in turn routed word of the sighting of the unknown vessel to Commissioner of Navigation Chamberlain in Washington. Sending it on up the line to Hoover's office, Chamberlain penned his brief analysis:

"Mr. Richey, I think this was probably a destroyer. ETC"

BITTER END ON THE *HARVESTER*
New York, New York
July 1, 1921

The Texas Oil Company's steamship *Harvester* lay at anchor off Isla de Lobos, south of Tampico, Mexico. Nine mutinous sailors crept up on the captain and assistant engineer and came against them with axes—but the two officers heard and saw them in just enough time to pull out their rifles and fire into the mob. Onrushing still, the sailors hacked the captain severely and disarmed both officers and might have murdered them, except for the wounded engineer's somehow getting hold of his rifle again and then backing the mutineers into the brig, the bleeding captain handcuffing them as he got them behind bars.

Once the brig door was slammed shut and locked, both captain and engineer passed out from loss of blood and in this state were found by other officers returning from shore leave.

Now the U.S. marshal in New York City anxiously awaited the *Harvester*'s imminent docking at Bayonne, New Jersey, where and when he would yank the nine out of their brig irons and thrust them toward arraignment, trial, and prison. Had the mutineers succeeded, said federal agents, then the *Harvester* might have joined the nation's purported fleet of mystery ships, its crew the newest crowd of high-seas pirates.

TWO SEAMEN SPECULATE

Boston, Massachusetts
July 1, 1921

Captain Wendell told the FBI here that Captain Willis Wormell was "known among shipping circles as a man of sterling character." His opinion of what had happened was clear and simple: Captain Wormell had died on the trip north from Brazil and was buried at sea. His death left an inexperienced crew sailing the ship, which to Wendell explained both the loss of anchors and the report that the *Deering* was, or seemed to be, in the charge of a foreigner when she sailed by the Lookout Shoals lightship. That these bad navigators grounded the ship on the Outer Diamond presented no mystery to him.

Earlier, in Portland, Maine, Captain Albert Frost had theorized that Captain Wormell and his crew made every effort—with all sails set—to work the *Deering* off the shoals, and then, having failed and fearing a storm might be approaching, they left in the ship's boats and drowned in the attempt to escape. "Now, we know that they would have been better off," said Captain Frost, "had they remained on board the vessel, but other vessels which have gone on Diamond Shoals have been pounded to pieces quickly and all hands lost."

MUTINY ON THE *POCAHONTAS*

American Consulate
Naples, Italy
July 7, 1921

On the 4th of July, the American steamer *Pocahontas* at last pulled into Naples after a lengthy and, at times, violent crossing from New York.

The American Consul quickly investigated an apparent mutiny involving the ship's foreign crew. Once she was eastbound and well out, some of the men threatened her captain and then went rampaging, wrecking her machinery and electric lighting—some said they were trying to sink the ship. Passengers volunteered, though, jumped in to help quell the riot and get the crippled ship into port. *Pocahontas* steamed on into St. Michael's in the eastern Azores and lay up there a good while for repairs.

By the time she reached Naples, her voyage had taken six long weeks.

COLLISION OFF CAPE HATTERAS

The Atlantic Ocean
60 miles south-southeast of Cape Hatteras
July 9, 1921

Off Diamond Shoals, a schooner as dark as the overcast night collided with the northbound Norwegian steamer *Fort Morgan* at nine o'clock in the evening, the schooner's high-pointing bowsprit raking and wrecking the entire superstructure of the *Fort Morgan*—bridge, mainmast, wheel- and charthouses, and funnel—and very nearly sinking her.

When the black mass rose over the steamship's port quarter, the watch yelled a warning, then saw a sailor with a red lantern running along the schooner's rail. Moments later came the crash, knocking the *Fort Morgan* way over on her beam—she recovered, only to have her deck swept and smashed by the bowsprit.

The mysterious schooner sailed away at once, incognito and incommunicado, answering none of the steamer's signals, and disappeared.

As the *Fort Morgan* approached New York a few days later, a Sandy Hook pilot said of her: "She's the most desolate craft that ever passed the Ambrose Channel lightship."

EYEING *CYCLOPS*

Washington, D.C.
July 10, 1921

Mystery piled upon mystery, and now an old, unsolved case was overlaying the new, as the *Washington Times* bannered: Phantom Pirate Ship May Be the Lost *Cyclops*—Crew May Hide Craft in Amazon.

Speculators the paper identified only as "government officials," still inspired by the implications of the Buxton note-in-a-bottle, held forth to the sensational press the latest notion toward identifying the oil-burning raider of late.

"Is the United States naval collier *Cyclops*, missing since 1918, the pirate vessel which has been ravaging Atlantic shipping for months?" asked the *Times*, and the question was well put indeed.

At 542' length overall and with a beam of 65', the collier *Cyclops* had been one of the largest American ships in service in the 1910s, launched at Philadelphia in May 1910 and sailing as part of the U.S. Navy Auxiliary Service, Atlantic Fleet, in November 1910.

The summer of 1911 saw her in the Baltic, supplying ships of the U.S. Navy's Second Division. She coaled the navy's patrols off Mexico during the revolutionary times of 1914 and 1915, even bringing a boatload of refugees out of Tampico and into New Orleans. Fully commissioned by the navy in May 1917, she convoyed to St. Nazaire on the coast of France, sailing back to America in July. The *Cyclops* steamed once that year to Nova Scotia but otherwise plied the eastern shipping lanes of the United States till the first of 1918, when she joined the Naval Overseas Transportation Service.

Returning from South America in March of '18, the *Cyclops* vanished.

Was she captured by Germans?

Or did the forty-seven life-term prisoners on board mutiny, killing captain and crew and turning to piracy, hiding up some South American river and going to sea infrequently and unpredictably, to raid and plunder, sallying forth to rove and prey upon slower, smaller sailing vessels just like the *Deering*?

Or had pirates from yet another vessel overcome the entire 306 crew and passengers?

Had some storm caught her and her cargo of manganese in the open ocean and broken and sunk her?

Did the life buoy found many miles northeast of Bermuda by the collier *Orion* when she retraced the *Cyclops*'s course come from the lost ship?

All that anyone could say for certain was that the collier *Cyclops* set out to sea from Rio de Janeiro on the 16th of February 1918, touched at

Barbados on the 3rd and 4th of March, and then disappeared. Some wonder, that was — her last two ports of call being Rio and Bridgetown.

Just like the *Carroll A. Deering*.

SUBJECT: BOTTLE

Department of Commerce
Washington, D.C.
July 18, 1921

From within Hoover's own department, the Bureau of Standards now brought forth for Lawrence Richey its clear and decidedly unmysterious analysis of the celebrated drift bottle from Buxton, North Carolina:

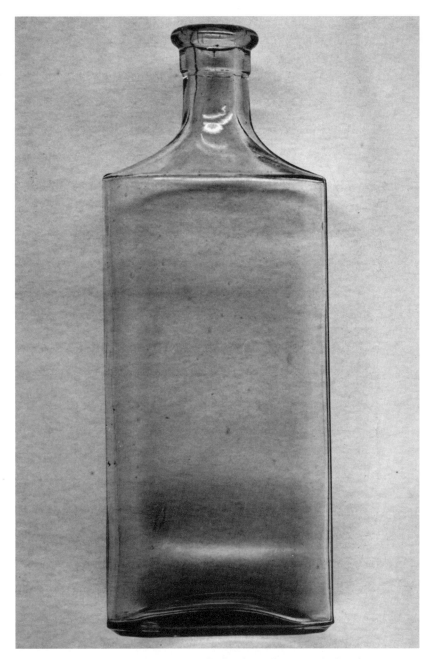

The bottle that fisherman Gray reported finding in April 1921 on the beach at Buxton, near Cape Hatteras, N.C., with a letter from the *Carroll A. Deering* inside

This bottle is similar in all particulars to the commonly made American bottle. It is generally known to the trade as a hand made twelve ounce Philadelphia improved oval prescription bottle, which is made in considerable quantities in the factories in the East and in San Francisco. Judging from the green color of the bottle it might possibly have been made on the Pacific Coast rather than in the East, as the Pacific Coast manufacturers use a great deal of beach sand, which only produces the green glass.

We have attempted to analyze what appeared to be a residue inside the bottle to determine whether or not this might be a residue from sea water. We, however, obtained no reactions indicating the presence of chlorides or sulfates which sea water is likely to contain. The only indications we got were that the solution is alkaline. On examining the more easily visible outlines of what appeared to be a residue in the bottle the lines show up as wrinkles or very fine cracks on the interior, in which small amounts of dirt appear to have been deposited. These wrinkles or cracks might easily have been there since the bottle was manufactured. Examinations of the exterior sides of the bottle with the hand glass indicated that all the roughness is due to mold marks rather than any grinding or etching with sand, as the bottom surfaces of the slight indentations are not roughened or etched.

We hope this report will assist you with your work.

F.C. Brown, For the Director

Even before this memorandum reached Richey, he had in his possession the Norfolk FBI man's narrative of July 9, in which the Coast Guard's division command there had observed of the bottle that it was neither *sand-pitted*, as it may well have been had it lain on shore for any length of time, nor *sunburned* from being exposed while floating in the water for the nine or ten weeks between the January 31 disappearance of the *Deering*'s crew and the April 10 discovery of the bottle by Christopher Columbus Gray.

Trying to learn more of drift-bottle behavior, Norfolk agent Kemon had even scoured the *Hydrographic Bulletin* for the past year, finding and forwarding these official records:

A bottle paper set adrift June 19th, 1919, at Latitude 33 degrees 45 minutes North, Longitude 76 degrees 10 minutes West, was recovered on Chesil Beach near Portland, Dorset, England, on July 2d, 1920; a bottle paper set adrift on September 22nd, 1920, at Latitude 37 degrees 7 minutes North, Longitude 75 degrees 24 minutes West, was recovered on Hog Island, Virginia, on October 3d, 1920; and a bottle paper set adrift on October 11th, 1920, at Latitude 30 degrees 15 minutes North, Longitude 70 degrees 16 minutes West, was recovered at Port Howe, Cat Island, Bahamas, on January 20th, 1921. These are all the recorded paper drifts in that vicinity.

These facts Hoover's sleuth found far more interesting than rumor and romance. The reports were indeed assisting Mr. Richey with his work.

CHRISTOPHER COLUMBUS GRAY
Buxton, North Carolina
Summer 1921

Mullet man, pure and simple, that's what I am now.

Oh, I'm not bragging. I'm not saying I'm wild about it, it's just what you end up doing most the time out here, if you can't get signed on with the government. Some of those boys, once they do, they got a lifetime lock on it, seems like.

It's one hell of a lot of fish in the sea—I was almost career navy, been all over so I can damn sure tell you *that*. One hell of a lot of fish, and most of em's mullet. You give me a buck for every mullet I've caught or eaten, and I could line em up end to end all the way from Hatteras Light to Jupiter. Sure could, and don't think I wouldn't, cause wouldn't *that* be a sight to see?

Only reason I'm out here splitting stovewood for the wife and ain't out there jumping mulleting right now is, well, they ain't jumping just this second. The boys that're out there setting nets, they're just burning daylight and killing time, far's I can see. Sure, they think they're going to fill a bunch of mullet barrels and be rolling in gold like Blackbeard, but they can go ahead and *try* to pull in five pounds this week and while they're at it, they can kiss my ass.

I like fishing, I really do, but you can stand right there on the beach, day like this, look out there and you know cause you can tell, you been around it all your life and you're raised to it, you can tell you're not going to do any good.

Where're you going to sell your catch anyway? We fish out here for a living, and then instead of spending some of that D.C. salary and buying from us and sending a little our way, what do the lighthouse folks and the Coast Guard boys do, but go out and fish for *themselves*! Hadn't folks ever heard of share the wealth?

So what kind of fool goes back on out when you know you gon get skunked? Some Kinnakeeter yaupon eater is what, some *damn* fool is what! My momma might've raised me to fish. She might even've raised me to be in the navy sailing around in tincans coaling their boilers and oiling their engines for all those years—you talk about *hot*, those damn engine rooms get what you call *real hot*! But she sure as hell didn't raise me to go out jumping mulleting when there ain't none running even if they do run most the time this time of year, and then what, be standing there in the skiff playing out net and have some rogue wave knock me out of the boat and tangle me up in my own net and drown me dead as a mackerel? I don't believe that's what Mr. Christopher Columbus Gray's momma had in mind, God rest her soul, and I ain't doing it.

I've really got to sharpen this hatchet—he is one dull sonofabitch. To do that I'll have to buy a sharpening stone and to buy a sharpening stone I'll be needing to sell fish to people who're not *buying*.

Too hot to fish, anyway, even if the damn mullet were running. Merkle bushes heating up, I can really smell em back here in the skeetery woods. I don't mind it either, not a bit, smells good, hot and waxy, like summertime's supposed to. But I do wish all those beetles and crickets would do me a favor ever now and then just shut the hell up.

And talk about hossflies! What good is a hossfly, I'd like to know? When we were boys, my cousin and I, we used to set in the door frame at home and roll up an old newspaper or two and pop hossflies with em. Whop em with an *Independent*, set em free from their awful hossfly lives! Get em with the *Advance* and send em on into the next world! I mean, we'd get to joking like that, carrying on, and it was some fun. And I tell you, anybody loves hossflies, that's one ill individual. Only good one's a dead one, and you know what, won't anything even eat it for bait—you can't even bait a hook with one of those sonofabitches!—not for anything lives around *here* anyway. Skeeters can bleed me all day long if they want to and that's what makes em happy, but Good Lord preserve us from hossflies. If they need a natural enemy and haven't got one yet, just say hey, and I'll be it.

One thing you *can* say about government work, though, is: every week they got to pay you—doesn't matter if you're the top dog or the fice, the eagle's gonna fly on Friday. Ten, twelve years in the navy'll get you used to that, so maybe something comes open, say, up here at the lighthouse, well, hell, they got my application papers—wouldn't take me anytime to get going on that project. Nobody needs to be looking any farther than me, just sign me up. Don't have to find me a place to live, cause here I already am—I like it here just fine, our little place right back of the beach. Edge of the woods, beach, it all runs together. Yeah, I like it all right, there just isn't hardly a dime to be had, and there sure as hell aren't two nickels a man can rub together, *nothing* except what washes up out of the sound or the sea.

And if it's mullet, then fine, by damn, let it be mullet. If it's flotsam on the tide, then I'll take flotsam. Or jetsam, I don't care. That's what happens to you, you stack up enough years in Uncle Sam's navy, and you start to feel like *you* might be something that's washed up, or that's just about to be.

Flotsam and jetsam, whoever heard of stuff like that in some real town upstate? Whoever heard of us or ever gave a damn about who we are or how we're living way out here in Buxton, North Carolina? Answer me that, now, I say, but you can't. There's smarter stuff washes up here every day—fruitbaskets and taterbarrels and driftwood—than the man who's sitting in the governor's mansion in Raleigh right now, whoever the hell *he* is.

Governor Fruitbasket.

Got *my* vote.

W. O. SAUNDERS

Offices of the Independent
505 East Fearing Street
Elizabeth City, North Carolina
July 1921

There's work to be done in this world, they say. And some days in the office I just have to sit back in this old cap'n's chair, listen to those old springs creak and stretch, put my feet up on the desk and my hands behind my head, and look out at all the sheer bustle in the street and down on the river and just plain marvel at what all we get done here in Betsy Town!

Why, when the Ides of April were barely upon us, the first May peas of the season were in the stores, grown right here in Mrs. George Twiddy's garden!

A week later, Mr. R. C. Abbott, the forwarding agent, was pushing his refrigerator iced cars for green peas. "Here Are My Connections," he advertised in the *Independent*, "You Can't Beat 'Em," and there he was, offering every truck farmer and market gardener in northeastern North Carolina outlets in New York City, Philadelphia, and Norfolk.

The week after *that*, he was getting five to seven dollars a basket for May peas! If turtles'll sit out sunning on a log around here—and they will—peas'll grow in springtime to beat the band! And you average, let's say, six dollars a basket, friend, that'll start to be some very nice folding money, yes, sir, it will.

Truck farming in Pasquotank's a going thing—from all over the Albemarle, just bring it in by wagon, sharpie, schooner, and whatever crop you got going, they'll freight it on up north that very day or the next.

By the first of July, Abbott was fairly shouting "Let Me Handle Your Potatoes," and, by my lights, he had something to shout about: "During the recent pea movement," he said, "I shipped 65 refrigerated carloads, twenty six thousand baskets, and never lost a basket."

Never lost a basket, not one! We're a shipping town, and our shipping works, whether it's by boats or trains. You have to like that percentage. You have to like those numbers. And everybody in Elizabeth City and all over the Albemarle just *has* to like Mr. R. C. Abbott.

LULA WORMELL

57 Lawn Avenue
Portland, Maine
July 1921

It has made my heart lift up, and it has given me hope, to see all these men go to work, to see what they are willing to do to find Father and the rest of the *Deering*'s crew.

Beyond that, think of what all the other families have been going through, those with missing fathers and brothers and sons and husbands, to wait not knowing anything at all of their fates, to wait in fear . . .

What of all those who *do* know where their loved ones are? Upon what ships and bound for what expected ports of call? As long as pirates are abroad, no one can rest comfortably—no one can for a moment believe any seaman is safe anywhere.

This is everyone's battle. As we are a maritime nation, this piracy affects us all, and no one is left untouched.

No one at all.

W. O. SAUNDERS

Offices of the Independent
505 East Fearing Street
Elizabeth City, North Carolina
Ides of July, 1921

Well, now, hear this.

Following on the heels of widespread conjecture of modern submarine piracy and numerous press accounts of "mystery ships," it now appears there are some who're going to try and wrest sunken treasure from the sea. A bunch of salvage outfits have gone and asked the Coast Guard and the Bureau of Navigation of the Department of

Commerce to furnish them with statistical data covering the cargo vessels lost along the Atlantic coast for the past fifty years.

Fifty years!

From what the old timers, all the old salts around Betsy and on down the sound, tell me, since the Civil War there haven't been but about *three hundred* or so shipwrecks around the Outer Banks of North Carolina alone! And that's just hereabouts—so it's a whale of a lot of statistics those salvors are asking for, and I wonder who's going to dig all that stuff up for them, and how much us taxpayers are going to be shelling out for it and on top of that why *should* we?

Read it in the papers:

"Salvage concerns making the request claim to have equipment and facilities for major salvage operations except in extreme depths. It is hoped to learn from the authorities the exact positions of sunken vessels and from their underwriters, the value and nature of the cargo laden. It is the intention of the salvers to raise the vessels when possible, and where this is impracticable, to recover the treasure."

Treasure! Everybody's always looking for some sort of treasure, seems like, looking for something and they don't know any more than Adam's all-purpose housecat what they're going to do with it when they find it—the whole world's searching for gold.

Or love.

Why, we've just had a case down in Dare County of love-seekers who actually succeeded, after their own fashion, and what a strange story it was, too.

She was in her forties, an artist's model, a chorine, a Broadway actress.

He was a young man of the Outer Banks.

And yet, and yet . . . how they did love! So attentive to her was he in the late summer of '20 that everyone in Nag's Head commented upon it, all their friends—and yet they were so surprised, that was the word that got back here, anyway, when she and young James Leary eloped.

By skiff they went off to Hatteras Island, where for months and months they lived out on that strip of beach, enjoying the life of romantics, near naturists, best anyone could tell. They walked the strand, they wet their lines for spot and pompano, they bathed in the ocean sea. To those who witnessed this pair of lovers it all seemed so idyllic.

But in this idyllic place she fell ill.

A doctor some miles away could not make his way to them quickly over sand-rut roads, and only an hour before the medic (this must have been the navy pharmacist's mate they call Doc Folb, for there isn't any *real* doctor out there), before he reached her, she died—her appendix, it was, ruptured and killed her.

Leary then borrowed a shad boat with which to bring her up to Elizabeth City for burial. And when that boat arrived here late last Saturday night, I tell you this was one weird spectacle to behold, coming up that dark Pasquotank River, up to the Water Street wharf—that young man, grief stricken, at the shad boat's tiller, with the body of his dead wife stretched across the bow.

I thought then I was seeing an omen.

And so I was.

GUMSHOE IN DARE COUNTY (II)

Hatteras Island, North Carolina
July 17–24, 1921

The Norfolk and Washington steamboat ferried Agent Harrie D. Knickerbocker down from the capital Sunday night, arriving at the Norfolk docks at 8 A.M. Monday morning. Over to Portsmouth Knickerbocker went, where he boarded the lighthouse tender *Columbine*, the craft regularly plying the waters between Hampton Roads, Virginia, and the lighthouses and light vessels of North Carolina's Outer Banks. The tender sailed from Portsmouth at 2 P.M., rounded Cape Henry, and after rough passage down the Banks anchored a mile off Hatteras Light 10 A.M. Tuesday the 19th. *Columbine* wirelessed Captain B. R. Ballance, keeper at Cape Hatteras, and presently Knickerbocker was fetched from the tender and brought ashore, where he made Coast Guard Station No. 183 his headquarters.

After dropping in on the C. C. Millers, the Buxton postmaster and his wife who both studied a photostat of the bottle message and as-

Hatteras Island, ca. 1900, view from aloft, U.S. Weather Signal Station, Hatteras, N.C.

sured the agent that none of their postal patrons had *that* handwriting, Agent Knickerbocker told Captain Ballance, "I want to see this man Gray."

"He's wild as a deer," Captain Ballance warned. "Best to get you into some old clothes, catch him off guard."

A little later, Christopher Columbus Gray stood in his yard and watched them as Ballance's car pulled up slowly and stopped at his gate. At first he showed no alarm, but when he acceded to Ballance's request that he come over to the car and then saw Knickerbocker, a stranger, he began shifting swiftly from side to side and would not look Knickerbocker in the eye.

"I'm from the Department of Commerce," the agent said. "Just trying to solve a few mysterious points in the *Deering* case."

"Well," said Gray, telling it yet again, "I was picking up driftwood along the shore and saw this bottle, must've just washed up cause it was still wet. Never seen a bottle before like the one I found, and haven't seen one like it since that one."

"How were you able to get the message out of it without tearing it?"

"You got any paper, I'll show you."

Knickerbocker reached for his briefcase in the backseat of the car, pulled out one piece of paper and handed it to the fisherman. Gray folded it, tore it into a half-sheet, rolled this into a small cone and said that the message had stood upright in that shape within the bottle, a small bit of it protruding up into the bottle's neck. He said he had carefully run a stick down into the inside of the paper cone and in that fashion withdrawn it from the bottle.

"That paper was damp, but it wasn't wet enough to tear when I pulled it out."

He's ill at ease with this, thought Knickerbocker. He'll talk to me if he's more at ease. Maybe get him to pose, appeal to his vanity . . . I've got my camera in the car.

"That's pretty good work. How about letting me get a picture of you, kind of showing how you did it? Be all right?"

"Oh, not in my old clothes here—I've got a good picture in the house I'll give you, just wait."

Gray then retreated the forty or fifty paces to his house and slipped inside. Presently his boy came forth and brought a photograph to Knickerbocker beside the car. Gray made himself scarce and failed to return, and, as Knickerbocker was sorely disappointed in not learning any more than he had, nothing more than Gray had several weeks earlier told Agent Thompson, he determined to give it another go the next day.

Back at the Cape Hatteras station, after dinner, Captain Ballance and Agent Knickerbocker sat and listened to the light, steady summer surf and talked some more about that bottle.

"Way I learned about it," Ballance said, "was this—Coast Guard headquarters in Norfolk sent me word, late April, said go see Christopher C. Gray and obtain a bottle and a message that Gray has found and written the Custom House about."

"And he turned it over to you, without any problem?" Knickerbocker asked.

"Not exactly. I drove my car over to Gray's place, told him what I

U.S. lighthouse tender *Columbine*, in service between Hampton Roads, Va., and Beaufort, N.C., in 1921. Length 155', beam 26'6", draft 12'3", 643 tons.

was there for, and he said, 'Well, I haven't got them—I threw the bottle and the message back out on the beach after I found it and read the message. But I'll go back to that same spot and see can I find them again.' And he did."

"He *did*?"

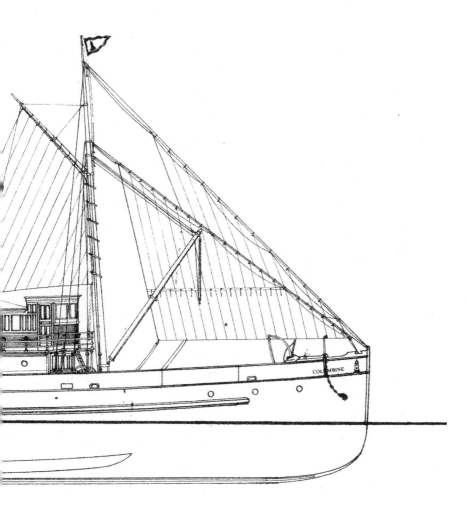

"Said he did."

"Found it a second time—on the seabeach?"

"Well, he came into the station here the next day and gave me the bottle and the message and told me he'd been lucky and they hadn't moved."

"Captain Ballance," Knickerbocker said. "The date on the Custom House letter is April 10th. The date they actually received it was April 18th. Let's say you got word and went over to Gray's that day or the day after, and then Gray has to go back and lay his hands on those curious items again, and then it's overnight before he comes to you with the goods. What're we up to?"

"Either the 19th or the 20th," Ballance said. "I sent them on to Norfolk."

"And from there they eventually came to us in Washington."

"One more thing, though."

"Yes?"

"After Gray left it with me, I got a good whiff of that bottle."

"Seawater, was it?" Knickerbocker asked.

"Whiskey," Captain Ballance replied.

Early the next morning, with Ballance and another Coast Guardsman and a different car from the one they had driven the day before, Knickerbocker proceeded again to Gray's Buxton home, or rather to a spot near it. While Ballance and Knickerbocker waited in the car, hidden several hundred feet short of Gray's place, the surfman walked on to the house, heard someone chopping wood, and asked Gray's wife— who met him at the front door—if he might see Mr. Gray.

"He's out back," she said. "The boy'll show you."

By the time the man and boy rounded the house, Gray had vanished, taken to the sandy woods and myrtle scrub where he evaded both the federal government, here now in the form of a surfman, and his own seven-year-old son, who only thought he was doing the right thing by helping the Coast Guard find his daddy. After three-quarters of an hour thrashing about in the bright, hot, summer-morning maritime woods, the two of them gave up the search, and when the surfman brought this sorry report back to his chief and the FBI agent, so, too, did they.

"Guess he's run out of things to say," Ballance mused.

"Yes, Cap'n," said Knickerbocker, "I guess he has. I reckon that, on *this* subject anyway, the old boy is just about talked out."

A MEETING AT MR. RICHEY'S OFFICE

Department of Commerce
19th and Pennsylvania Avenue, NW
Washington, D.C.
July 25, 1921

On the morning of Saturday, July 23, at a quarter till ten, Lawrence Richey had inquired by phone of the Commerce Department's Bureau of Lighthouses as to the whereabouts of the bureau's lighthouse tender *Columbine*. Richey had expected to have heard already from the most recent Department of Justice man who had traveled on board *Columbine* to Cape Hatteras, investigating the strange case of the *Deering*.

In fifteen minutes, the bureau called Richey back, reporting that the vessel carrying the agent from Justice was due "tomorrow or Monday," its "return delayed by storm off Hatteras." What Richey was about to learn from his counterpart at Justice was a fact, or facts, the knowledge of which would demand Richey's personal attention and, indeed, would compel him to sail to Cape Hatteras, where he could see and hear of these matters for himself.

A key meeting in the case of the *Carroll A. Deering* took place this last Monday in July. In attendance were Lawrence Richey, Mr. Pinkerton for the State Department, Mr. Evans for Justice, Mr. Maxam and Captain Henderson for the Coast Guard, and Harrie D. Knickerbocker for the FBI; the latter (having returned to Portsmouth aboard the *Columbine* at Sunday noon, caught the 4:15 P.M. Chesapeake Bay steamer, and gotten back into the capital at midnight) gave a fresh report about his just-completed trip to the Outer Banks.

Nowhere, Knickerbocker said—not in four stores at Buxton, or in others at Ocracoke village, and significantly not among the fifty bottles and jars of the *Deering*'s salvaged medicine chest—had he seen any bottles or any paper that resembled the drift bottle and its letter. All the interviews on this point had gained him no information, beginning with his first inquiry of Buxton's postmaster and his wife, whom Agent Knickerbocker deemed not "very conversant on 'bottle-ology.'"

"What about this man Gray, then?" Richey pressed. "What do you make of him?"

"Captain Ballance at the Cape station called him 'wild as a deer,' and he's not far wrong," the agent said. "He cut the talk short one evening, and ran off into the woods and swamps when we came back the next day. Nothing I did should've made him act that way."

"Your being there was enough, sounds like," Richey said. "Anything else?"

"Well, when I was talking with the wreck commissioner at Cape Hatteras, a fellow named Gaskill, he said he didn't know Gray well, but thought he had a good reputation. Said the only thing he'd ever heard against Gray was that when he was a boy, he had a habit of writing notes to girls and dropping them along the road for the girls to pick up."

"Do tell."

"Seems Gray's had a 'note-writing habit' for quite a while," Agent Knickerbocker said.

"*Seems*, Harrie?" Richey stirred, rose from behind his desk. "Soon as I can, I'll go down there, before the end of August, for sure. And we'll just see about him."

A SUSPECT IN BEAUFORT
Beaufort, North Carolina
Summer 1921

Albert I. Lewis of Beaufort, North Carolina, having followed the sea for nearly twenty years, had quit the sailor's life and was now settled ashore in this little port of the central coast, where he advertised himself as a marine underwriters' agent, general stevedore and contractor, and dealer in steam and domestic coal.

Lewis's late-winter letter to Captain Jacobson of Lookout Shoals light vessel, asking for details of the *Deering* when she passed there on January 29, had gotten Jacobson into hot water, for Jacobson on the Ides of March had answered Lewis guilelessly, citing *Light Vessel No. 80*'s log. Reprimanded from higher up in the Bureau of Lighthouses for this divulgence, Captain Jacobson later had waited nearly two months to respond to Lula Wormell's mid-May query seeking more information than he had given Lewis. When he did answer her, it was only after he had reported his story in a hearing before the Bureau in Washington, and his July 10 note to Miss Wormell merely referred her to the Superintendent of Lighthouses in Baltimore, Maryland.

As the summer of '21 progressed, no fewer than three FBI agents inquired around about the character and judgment of this Albert Lewis, and at least two of the three called upon him to interview him in person.

First, Agent Kemon picked up word that Lewis was a busybody who, in addition to his maritime business, filed Carteret County reports for several out-of-town newspapers. "It is just possible," Kemon observed, "that Mr. Lewis might have written this bottle message, and placed it where it would have been picked up—in all probability by some one of the Coast Guard—and the news value of this find would be good copy for him. It is suggested that Mr. Lewis's handwriting be compared with that of the bottle message."

Agent Thompson then dropped in on Mr. Lewis and found him to be a great talker. Lewis said he'd heard from Captain Carlson of the wrecking tug *Rescue*, who led the assay of the *Carroll A. Deering* on the 4th of February and who told Lewis that the boats' ropes were rounded back to the davits and that to him the ship looked plundered. Lewis let Thompson know he was certain the crew had mutinied and taken everything off the *Deering* in the ship's power boat, which the seas promptly swamped, drowning all hands.

When he tried Lewis's ideas out on Captain Goodwin of the Coast Guard, though, Agent Thompson heard nothing but skepticism— doubt that it would even be possible to launch the ship's boats while foundered on the Outer Diamond, doubt that the power boat could be effectively maneuvered around the grounded ship, doubt that the mutinous crew could carry very much of the *Deering*'s gear and equipment in the boat, and extreme doubt that from the boat the crew could somehow have rounded the davit falls back up.

Agent Knickerbocker arrived in Beaufort on the afternoon of Thursday, July 21, introducing himself to Albert Lewis as a special representative of the Department of Commerce. To Knickerbocker, Lewis speculated: If the mystery steamer that approached the Lookout Shoals lightship (and then quickly retreated from it, ignoring the lightship's calls) were a British tramp, then that was no wonder at all—for, in his experience, British ships never paid any attention to such signals. He also posited the *Deering* might have lost both anchors due to the failure of a weak link connecting both anchor chains at the near end—the engineer's using too much power in weighing the anchors could have broken that weak link, he thought. (Knickerbocker would shortly put this notion to other seafaring men, none of whom bought it.)

Nothing the FBI man suggested on the spot could entice Lewis to write anything down. Finally, Knickerbocker resorted to flattery, telling him that Secretary of Commerce Hoover and his assistant had taken a strong personal interest in the *Deering* and that they would value highly Lewis's opinions on the case. Would he write them? Yes, Lewis agreed, he would.

His main theories about the *Deering* may have been debunked, but the old mariner's word was bond. He penned a short letter to Lawrence Richey the next Tuesday, saying he would write more soon "and give you the facts in the case as far as I know." Back in Washington when Lewis's letter reached Richey, Agent Knickerbocker, upon seeing it, quickly judged that Lewis's handwriting was "not at all similar" to that of the bottle message.

Albert Lewis, without knowing he had risen to bait and bitten, was now off the FBI hook and could keep on dealing in steam and domestic coal, no longer a suspect, forever unaware.

A CLUE IN PORTUGAL?

American Consulate General
Lisbon, Portugal
July 27, 1921

Into the Consulate General on this day marched a sailor named Augusto Frederico Martins. He presented a Portuguese passport issued in Glasgow, Scotland, the previous May, and he wished to be signed on the articles of the outward-bound American steamship *West Maximus*. Consul General Stanley Hollis looked him over and thought it at least slightly curious that, though Martins appeared to be an able-bodied seaman, he wished to sign on beneath his rank.

With more curiosity, though, Consul Hollis regarded this man against the description of an "A. Martins" from the crew list of the *Hewitt* and found the resemblance of the *Hewitt*'s crewman and the man before him to be "rather" close.

"And where have you sailed recently?" asked the consul.

"Brazil," Martins admitted. "And Argentina."

"Then you arrived in Glasgow," said Consul Hollis.

"Yes."

"How did you come to be there?"

"Why, by ship, of course."

"By what ship, sir?" the consul continued.

"She was Portuguese," said the sailor.

"There are many Portuguese ships, Mr. Martins. What was the name of your ship?"

The sailor said nothing, and to Consul Hollis he seemed overall to be noncommittal and at times even contradictory. At length Martins spoke:

"Well, then, I was left there in Glasgow by a Portuguese ship from Oporto."

"You are certain?"

"Yes."

"Yet you have no papers?"

"I have my passport. I've shown you that."

"You have no ship's papers?"

"I have none, sir."

"Even so, Captain Jamison will sign you on as second cook, then, will he?"

"Yes, sir."

"You look to be an able-bodied seaman, and yet you're willing to accept the lesser position of second cook?"

"Captain Jamison needs no other services, sir."

"Very well," said the consul. "You're not the first seaman to lose his papers. You may sign the articles for the *West Maximus*, but do not lose *these* papers. Someone else will have you deported, or locked up, one."

Consul Stanley Hollis hoped he had not aroused the seaman's suspicions, and he cabled the secretary of state in Washington that evening with his report of this interview. The next day he sent dispatches concerning Martins to his consular counterparts in both Scotland and Brazil, noting the coincidences of the U.S. Navy collier *Cyclops* having disappeared on a voyage from Rio de Janeiro to the United States and the *Carroll A. Deering*'s crew, also voyaging from Rio to North America, having vanished.

Hollis's final remark was simply that the *West Maximus*—upon which the possible *Hewitt* seaman A. Martins shipped, if in fact he *was* the man who presented himself in Lisbon as Augusto Frederico Martins—had just cleared Lisbon bound for—where else?—Rio de Janeiro.

A CREWMAN FOUND
Department of Justice offices
New York, New York
August 1, 1921

At last one of the missing crew turned up.

Not from among the *Carroll A. Deering*'s crew, though, but instead a man from the sulfur steamship *Hewitt* that had sailed up the southeast coast not far behind the *Deering*, and that many believed may have retrieved the *Deering*'s crew, adrift on the open ocean in the ship's boats. The *Hewitt* was the ship that many also thought might have exploded off the New Jersey coast, possibly the source of the February 1 flash of light seen there.

The sailor's name was Bates Raney, and did he ever have a tale to tell the FBI.

Just before Christmas 1920, Raney, an Oklahoma City boy twenty-three years old and single, had signed on as third engineer with the *Hewitt* when she was anchored at the Maine Central Dock in Portland and shipped out on her to Texas. On the day she left Sabine, Texas, he had gone to take a look at a broken ice machine, smelled cyanide of potassium fumes in the ice-machine room, and bolted—but the gas he had already breathed knocked him out, and he fell from the top grating in the ship's engine room to the engine below.

Raney was taken off the ship just twenty minutes before she sailed on January 20, 1921.

He lay in Lakeview Hospital at Port Arthur for a week, his back badly sprained, then went to recuperate at his father's place in Denver, where the next thing he knew a reporter for the Associated Press called on him to ask about the *Hewitt*, which had mysteriously disappeared. From the wire-service man, Raney learned that she was lost and believed sunk.

Raney's father died, and Raney stayed just long enough to settle the estate and then moved on, first to Oklahoma City, thence to New York, where he boarded the Union Sulphur Company's SS *Herman Frasch* as second engineer. His next ship, also as a second, was the *Mopang*, which sailed from army base Pier 2 in Brooklyn, New York, for Bizerte, Tunisia, North Africa, where she took on oil and then stood for Constantinople. From there, she made for Derindje, Turkey, unloaded flour and clothing for the Near East relief effort and took on refugees, then headed back to Constantinople. The *Mopang* steamed through the Straits of Bosporus, hit a mine in the Black Sea just before dawn on June 30, and sank in six minutes.

All thirty-nine men, officers and crew, made it. They rowed in lifeboats into Burgas, Bulgaria, where they were put up in a hotel for four days and then sent on their way aboard the Bulgarian steamer *Czar Ferdinand* to Constantinople, where the American consul billeted them in a hotel for five more days. Next they took a small Greek ship to Polynos and Piraeus, Greece, boarding the *Megali Hellas* as consul passengers bound for New York City, stopping on the way only in Patras.

Safe now in New York, Raney recalled for Special Agent M. J. Drennan a conversation between the *Hewitt*'s captain and a Sabine pilot who had remarked upon coming aboard, "Very heavily loaded, aren't you, Captain," to which the captain replied, "I know it—it's the Company's orders and I have to do it or I'll lose my job."

"The supposition," Agent Drennan asked Raney, "is that she struck a mine?"

"No," said Raney. "My personal opinion is that she broke in two. I know she had been overloaded a couple of times. The officers at the mess table joked about it. The third mate said, 'We will all wake up some day and find ourselves floating in the Atlantic.'"

THE OCEAN CHART

57 Lawn Avenue
Portland, Maine
August 6, 1921

Now the *Deering*'s ocean chart was in Mrs. Wormell's hands, thanks to Lula and her trip to Washington, for it was Lawrence Richey who sent it their way. And once she had the chart, Mrs. Wormell could put it before someone whom she felt would understand its language and message better than anyone else, a peer. For if Captain Wormell were indeed one of the best and best known of America's schooner masters—and he was—to do him justice she would need the eyes and attention of another from that select company, another great sea captain.

That man was Frank Hewitt Peterson, who had captained the *Edward J. Lawrence*, a six-master built by Gardiner Deering's Bath rival Percy & Small not long after that firm had also constructed Captain Wormell's earlier command, the six-master named the *Alice M. Lawrence*. Captain Peterson had sailed the *Edward J. Lawrence* from New York to the Bay of Biscay during the Great War, carrying shell casings to the fight against the Germans. Then, homeward bound a couple of hundred miles west of France, he learned by radio that he was sailing directly toward a German U-boat and so shifted course for the northwest, making the journey to Hampton Roads by way of Newfoundland and avoiding the fate of his fellow traveler, the schooner *Carl F. Cressy*, which was under way without a wireless aboard and was thus unwarnable and got herself caught by the German submariner and sunk.

Captain Peterson had known Captain Wormell since the latter was master of the *Florence*, a three-masted schooner trading to Demerara, British West Indies, and importing asphalt from Trinidad. He had followed Wormell as captain of the four-masted *Alicia B. Crosby* when Wormell moved on to the five-masted *Nathaniel Palmer*, and he had watched Wormell's career as it led him next to the ill-fated *Alice M. Lawrence* and then to yet another five-masted schooner, the *Singleton Palmer*. Captain Peterson remembered Captain Wormell as "a very able master."

Mrs. Wormell and Captain Peterson pored over and over the *Carroll A. Deering*'s ocean chart, following Captain Wormell's penciled markings of his noon position each day, to the point that his hand stopped making the northward record of the doomed ship's last sail—January 23, a week before she foundered. Captain Peterson's conclusion at the time would never leave him, for much later in Boston, nearly thirty years after the wreck, after he had long since retired from the sea and become secretary of the Boston Marine Society, he would say to a sleuthing writer with total conviction the very same words he now spoke to the wife of Captain Wormell:

"Some other man recorded the last few days of the *Deering*'s voyage. Of that I am sure."

WORD ABOUT HAITI, JUST IN FROM BRAZIL

Aboard the SS Lake Fariston
Para, Brazil
August 11, 1921

Captain W. B. Hudgins, master of the steamship *Lake Fariston*, sat down in his cabin and drafted a letter to George Pickerell, the American consul in Para, to confirm their conversation of two weeks earlier, writing:

While Master of the SS *Elmac* en route from Europe to Puerto Plata, Haiti, I sighted a suspicious looking craft twenty miles North-east of Samana Bay, Haiti. This was at 11:00 P.M. on January 27th, 1921, a clear moonlight night.

The vessel, about the size of an American destroyer, was apparently making twenty knots. She showed no lights of any kind, and refused to answer my numerous signals. She passed me about a half-mile away, and disappeared over the Eastern horizon.

On my arrival in Puerto Plata, I reported the incident to the Ship's Agent, who said that the mysterious vessel was probably hunting smugglers.

Consul Pickerell sent the captain's report to the secretary of state's office in Washington, which later passed it over to the Bureau of Navigation in Commerce, noting that it was "in regard to the strange actions of a steamer off the coast of Haiti, in January of this year. Possibly this vessel has nothing to do with the accident to the *Carroll A. Deering* but I take the liberty of forwarding the letter as it may serve to reinforce other testimony you now have on hand.

"I have of course examined the crew lists of the various vessels demanding the service of this office," Pickerell continued, "and beg to state that several of the Captains with whom I conversed relative to the matter were surprised to learn of this 'mystery' ship and stated that they were under the impression that the accidents referred to were caused by storms or collisions at sea."

Was this ship yet another candidate for the piratical marauder, beyond the *Cyclops* and the recalcitrant, uncommunicative steamer Captain Jacobson of the Lookout Shoals lightship had spotted just after the *Deering* passed by there on January 29?

Or was this steamer possibly the very same vessel that Jacobson saw?

At top speed, if indeed twenty knots *were* her maximum, could she, in less than forty-eight hours, have stood for Carolina from Haiti and made it to a point anywhere close to the capes?

Could she?

W. O. SAUNDERS

Offices of the Independent
505 East Fearing Street
Elizabeth City, North Carolina
Mid-August 1921

Yes, you caught me at it again. I *do* like to lean back in my old captain's chair here in the office. Like to hear those old ungreased springs creaking and straining cause they always get me to thinking.

Thinking? I mean! I will pure-t wrap my brain around a mystery, now, puzzle it till it's about slam wore out, and here's where I've gotten to today on this *Deering* business.

Coal is the key.

Coal? you say. Well, yes. *And how's that, exactly?*

Can't say how, just yet. But it seems like everywhere you look, coal, King Coal sat right in the very middle of the matter.

Starting with, the only reason there still *were* any of these big-schooner colliers like the *Carroll A. Deering* was the coal boom during the war—they tell me that six years ago they were moving coal up our east coast for seventy-five cents a ton, and then all of a sudden South America can't get it from Europe anymore and has to look up thisaway and before too long these big schooners are loading up and heading for Rio and charging nearly seventeen *dollars* a ton. That's pretty easy math, even for a small-town newspaper editor.

Think of it—the collier *Cyclops*, missing, same route as the *Deering*, too—Rio to Barbados to, well, that's what we don't know. Coal coming down from the West Virginia coalfields by train to Norfolk, to go out by Hampton Roads . . . and the strike against Big Steel and the coal strike where nearly half a million miners laid out of work . . . the big-time coal man sitting there in J. P. Morgan's offices when the bomb went off across the street last September, and him saying right off it was Bolshevists . . . the *Carroll A. Deering* shipping coal to Brazil on her last outing . . .

Yep, you bet—coal was everywhere in this thing, through and

through. And she was on her way back to Hampton Roads for more, I reckon.

So what? I know—she didn't *have* any coal coming north. Of course pirates weren't going to hold her up and hijack her for coal she didn't have, if it were pirates, anyway. Or maybe it was pirates, except that the pirates and the able-bodieds working the *Deering* were one and the same, and the plunder they wanted was the same plunder they'd gotten aboard back in Barbados without Cap'n Wormell seeing it or knowing about it. A few cases of liquor, a few barrels of rum, maybe even *quite* a few.

An honest collier'd be a pretty good disguise for a rumrunner, wouldn't she, now? She couldn't outrun the Coast Guard, that's for sure, but, then again, she wouldn't *have* to. Who'd ever suspect her?

And a Hampton Roads coal dock would be kind of a dark, quiet, un-populated place if you wanted to roll those barrels off the ship in the dead of night.

And since almost everybody on the ship had signed on right there in Hampton Roads, chances are they'd know a blind tiger or two that'd be interested in Barbadian imports, especially if they were sampling the wares during normal business hours, which is to say two or three A.M.

So that's what these squeaky springs're telling me today. That's how coal figures into it. Coal is big business. America's business. And the biggest coal port in eastern America is right up on the north side of that Great Dismal Swamp yonder—Norfolk, Portsmouth, Newport News, Hampton Roads—World's Greatest Harbor!

Say what you will.

Coal is a nice, dark cover.

RUMRUNNING ARMADA

Chesapeake Bay
August 1921

Five schooners, with crews totaling fifty men and liquor aboard worth a quarter-million dollars, slipped past the Coast Guard's cutter *Manning* off the Virginia capes and on into Chesapeake Bay one

Monday night in August, but federal prohibition agents then laid a cordon of boats from Cape Henry to Cape Charles and bottled up the rumrunning armada in the bay.

From Maine to Miami, prohibition officers had recently let it be known they believed the mystery ships reported hither and yon were simply blockade runners filled with cargoes of liquor. The feds knew the names of the vessels, the identities of their masters, even how much whiskey was being consigned to a Richmond rumlord, all because one sailor in the bootlegger's paradise of Nassau, his lips loosened by ware sampling as he helped load the first 1,100 cases transshipped there from a converted submarine chaser, started freely telling the tale.

Hard liquor was all over Nassau, thousands of cases stored in warehouses and homes, stashed in hotels, cellars, and caves, just waiting to be shipped to the States by spindling sloops and former subchasers, by sharp launches sporting mahogany cabins and burnished brass, and by hundred-ton Grand Banks schooners that had deserted the fishing fleet and now wore tarpaulins over their sterns, covering their names. Once again, there was an air of piracy about the Bahamas, and smuggling was hereabouts a legitimate line of work.

Many trips they had made, the sailor said, the schooners all with auxiliary engines sneaking into the creeks and coves of the great Chesapeake estuary and loading their contraband off onto barges that were then heaped with hay and towed on up the bay.

Strong drink is worth a lot of loot, fifteen bucks a case, yeah, a lot of money, sang the sailor, and money is a good soldier, and will on.

MR. RICHEY ON THE OUTER BANKS
Cape Hatteras, North Carolina
August 1921

Late afternoon on August 16, 1921, Richey again telephoned the Bureau of Lighthouses, which had been trying for weeks now to coordinate this trip for him to North Carolina's sound country. He expected to leave Washington, Richey said, on the next evening's Norfolk and Washington steamboat passage. That being the case then, the bureau's plan for him would be as follows: On the morning of August 18, when the steamboat pulled into Norfolk, he could expect to be met there at the commercial dock by the *Columbine*, and aboard her take the outside trip to Buxton. As the *Columbine* would, weather permitting, return to Norfolk August 21 in time for Hoover's man to catch the return boat to the capital that evening, the lighthouse tender's trip south would allow Lawrence Richey two days in and around Cape Hatteras, two days to speak with any of the Coast Guard station crews he wished, or with the keepers of Hatteras Light, and, certainly, time enough to speak at length with the man who had turned up one of the most interesting, oft-quoted, and alarming communications of 1921, he of the manuscript-found-in-a-bottle, Mr. Christopher Columbus Gray.

To Buxton, once he had reached Cape Hatteras and enlisted the help of both Coast Guard and lighthouse crews, Lawrence Richey sent word that Mr. Gray should come at once to Hatteras Light to discuss Gray's application to work in the lighthouse service. Then Richey, wearing his fedora and dark, broad-lapel suit and tie even in August — he had the same broad face as Hoover — awaited Gray at the light itself, in the late afternoon on the porch of the keeper's house.

Richey was a man handy with hook and line — counting among his comraderies the Izaak Walton League, the Chicago Rod and Gun Club, and the Texas Blockhouse Fishing Club — and, as his bait was good, he was not disappointed. In a dingy broadcloth shirt and denim overalls, moving with languor through the thick summer, fisherman Gray shambled into view, crossing the sandspur yard and bound for the thin, swirled spindle of Hatteras Light.

"You there," Richey called from the keeper's porch.

Gray turned toward him, shoulders first, regarded him dully, and said, "You wanting me?"

"Perhaps — what's your name?"

"Gray."

"You're here about the lighthouse job, then," Richey said.

"Are you the man I talk to?"

"That I am."

"Well, I'm glad," said Gray, walking to the edge of the porch. "I was beginning to think I'd never hear back about it."

"I'm Lawrence Richey, Department of Commerce. Before we talk about the job, Mr. Gray, I need to clear up a few things with you about the schooner *Carroll A. Deering*."

At this word, Gray kicked the sand and rasped out, "I don't know what I can tell you, Mr. Richey, that I haven't already told the Coast Guard and the FBI."

"Sit down, please," said Richey. The two men sat on the porch steps, and Richey produced from his inside breast pocket several folded pages, photostatic copies of the bottle letter and of two letters Gray had written back in the spring, handing them to Gray. "Tell me what you make of these documents."

Gray scarcely gave them a glance. "Don't make anything of em— couple letters I wrote, and the note I found in the bottle down the beach there." He pointed off vaguely to the southwest.

"Come along, then," said Richey, "and show me where."

"That's three miles away from here, Mr. Richey."

"I doubt that."

"What do you mean?"

"Just this—there was no bottle and note till you wrote this letter to the Custom House in Norfolk. When they asked Captain Ballance to come and get it from you, you gave him that cock-and-bull story about how you'd thrown it back on the beach but you'd go to that spot and see if you could find it again. And then you had to produce them, and so that's what you sat down and did."

"I don't have to be a party to this," Gray fumed. "What makes you think you know so much?"

Again Lawrence Richey reached for his inside pocket, this time pulling forth typescripts. "Because I do."

Gray blanched when he saw the letterhead, the eagles with arrows in their claws, and knew then that it was all over. Behind them, the salt seawind was playing gaily with the white curtain over one of the keeper's windows, kicking it against the windowlight.

"Mr. Gray," Richey went on. "These two reports came to me from the best handwriting men in the Treasury and the United States Navy, and they state conclusively that the author of all three letters you now hold in your hand is you yourself and no one else. Not Herbert Bates. Not anyone from the *Deering*'s crew. This note—this whole episode, in fact—is a fraud. You've been running your government around in circles, Mr. Gray, for over four months now, isn't that correct?"

"Damn it!" Gray erupted bitterly, quickly rising—whereupon Richey grabbed his forearm and yanked him back down.

"Nobody ever tell you," Lawrence Richey said, "that innocent men don't run?"

In a heartbeat at Hatteras, Christopher Columbus Gray was caught, exposed, broken. There on the lighthouse keeper's porch, the fisherman began to cry. "It's true," said the weeping man, "it's true it's true it's all true. Just let me go and I'll give you everything I got." He dropped his head to his knees and swayed in misery, as wild, uproarious visions tormented him—he saw himself hanging from the upper railing of Hatteras Light, or from a yardarm high on a square-rigger's mainmast.

"You've got nothing I want," Richey said, "except your confession."

"It was my cousin's doing. He put me up to it."

"I don't believe that for a minute," Richey said. "For God's sake, man, tell the truth." The muddy fisherman sat and swayed in abject sorrow, and at last Lawrence Richey got what he'd sought for nearly three months, as the whole sorry truth of the matter finally came to light.

"They wouldn't buy our fish," Gray said.

"*What?*"

"All these men," Gray said, sweeping his hand around broadly in an arc from the lighthouse toward the Coast Guard station. "All of em on the federal payroll, and they never would buy from us—no, they'd go out and catch their own fish when here they had money to burn and us none."

So Gray wanted to join them, to get back on the government payroll he had enjoyed through three navy terms, and he had applied for a job in the lighthouse service. But he did not leave it at that, instead devising a simple, insidious plan to discredit the staff at Cape Hatteras Light in hopes of getting somebody fired, and then with his own appointment to fill the vacancy he himself had caused. The wreck of the *Carroll A. Deering* would be his tool, the way Gray figured it, believing back in April that, since neither Coast Guard nor lighthouse men had yet solved the case of the *Deering*, he as finder of such a key and central message as the note in the bottle could then march forth and make his way to higher figures in the federal government, emboldened by the information in his possession, and in the process cast a bad light on the men of the lighthouse and the surf stations.

Christopher Columbus Gray, namesake of a great sailor and discoverer, was himself a knave and a fool, one whose duplicitous act had taken from so many men and women that which he could never repay—their time, and even more than time, their spirit and hope in the cause of unraveling the mystery and solving this strange case.

Gray's one single dramatic lie had spent the strength of many hearts.

And so it was that the international alarm Gray had caused over piracy along the American east coast shipping lanes ended exactly where it began, at Buxton, at Cape Hatteras. Yet the mystery of the *Carroll A. Deering* that also began there did not, likewise, now end.

As to Gray's fate, he would not be prosecuted, Lawrence Richey said, once he got back to Washington and revealed to the press what had happened out on the beach at Buxton, and what most assuredly had *not*. He doubted whether there was any existing law under which the fisherman could be punished for the hoax, by his pronouncement in effect letting Gray's fraud stand as a weird, dark joke on the entire American government. According to the *Washington Post*, officials in various departments involved in the investigation of the *Deering* mystery were startled to learn Gray's message was a fake, but, whether from strain or bizarreness or the pent energy this cloudy and inconclusive story still held, these men of government, the newspaper said, "could only give vent to bursts of laughter."

Hatteras Light, Cape Hatteras, N.C., seen eight years after Lawrence Richey and Christopher Columbus Gray met here in August 1921

HANDWRITING (II)

The most damning documents Lawrence Richey had carried with him on this decisive trip to Dare County, North Carolina, were fresh ones, less than three weeks old, and they sealed the case that the

FBI agents had been piecing together all this summer against fisherman Gray.

Special Agent Harrie D. Knickerbocker had, on the day after the July 25 meeting in Richey's office, received the original April letter Gray wrote to the U.S. Custom House in Norfolk. He had already shown photostats of Gray's May letter to the U.S. Navy, seeking to reenlist, to the men at that July 25 meeting. "After making a close study of the handwriting of Mr. Gray in his letter to the Custom House," Knickerbocker had stated to Richey, "the writer is more convinced than ever that Gray wrote the bottle message. However, I intend to place the original bottle message and the originals of these two letters above mentioned before a handwriting expert within the next few days and we will await his decision."

Two experts, to be precise—one in the Navy Department's Bureau of Navigation, the other within the Treasury Department—both of whom were as fleet as they were decisive.

In an August 1 "Memorandum for Mr. Knickerbocker," the navy's J. H. Taylor stated at the outset:

In my opinion the "bottle letter" was written by Christopher Columbus Gray of Bixton, N.C. From examination of his letter dated April 10th, 1921, and the "bottle letter," I find the following characteristics on which my opinion is based:

1. The word "crew" in the "bottle letter" and "crew" in his letter of April 10th appear to me to have the same muscular movement and formation.

2. The letter "e" in the word "escape" and the letter "e" in the word "ashore" in his letter of April 10th has the same slant, shading and pressure at the end of the letter.

3. The letter "m" in "something" in the "bottle letter" and the letter "m" in the word "custom" in his letter of April 10th has the same shading, formation and particularly has the appearance of a small "e" at the end of this letter.

4. The letter "g" in "burning" in the "bottle letter"and the letter

Buxton. N.C.
April 10 1921

To U S Castoue House
Norfolk Va

Dear Sir

If you know any
thing of the Head quarters or
ouners of the six master
Schooner Carooll A Deering that
came ashore on Dimonds shoals
I wish you uould notify them
that I have found a letter
on a balle on Cape Hatiras
Beach telling how the ship
came to be lost from one of
the crew for infarmation

over

Deering captured by Oil Burning Boat something like chaser taking off everything hooptuing crew trese hiding all over ship no chance to make escape finer please notify head officer of Deering

The bottle letter

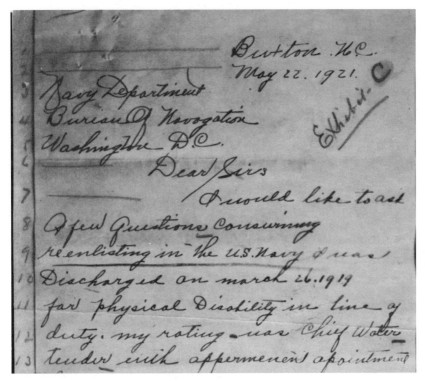

Gray's letter to Navy Department, Washington, D.C., May 22, 1921,
seeking reenlistment

"g" in "telling" in his letter of April 10th has the same formation and shading.

5. The word "of" in the "bottle letter" and the word "of" in his letter of May 22d, 1921 to the Bureau of Navigation, I find has the same general formation and shading.

6. The letter "t" in the word "capture" in the "bottle letter" and the letter "t" in the word "custom" in his letter of April 10th—I find that this letter is crossed above the letter in the same place on both the "bottle letter" and in his letter of April 10th. The letter "t" in "everything" in the "bottle letter" and the letter "t" in the word "them" in his letter of April 10th, 1921, has the same general formation and shading.

7. The letters "ip" in the word "ship" in the "bottle letter" and "ip" in "ship" in his letter of April 10th, have the same formation and shading.

8. The letter "n" in the word "no" in the "bottle letter" and the "n" in the word "notify" in his letter of April 10th, 1921, has the same formation and shading.

A Treasury Department typescript dated August 3, 1921, and titled *Memorandum for the Chief of Secret Service* compared the bottle letter with the same pair of documents as the navy's man had done—different from those the Portland handwriting teachers had worked with in May—and the rigorous eyes of Treasury's inspector revealed a truth the earlier readers in Portland were apparently not even looking for, and reached a vastly different conclusion indeed:

There has been referred to me for determination in handwriting, a document referring to the supposed capture of the Schooner "Carroll A. Deering," reading "Deering captured by oil burning boat, etc." With this reference I find a latter dated Buxton, N.C., April 10th, 1921, signed Christopher C. Gray, also a photograph of a letter dated May 22d, 1921, signed by Christopher Columbus Gray of the same place, these two specimens to be used as a standard of comparison in an effort to determine the identity of the person writing the message. For reference, I have marked the three specimens "Exhibits A, B [the Bottle Message] and C."

I have made a careful examination of the three exhibits and it is my opinion that they are all in the hand of the same person. In support of this opinion, the following analysis is submitted:

Physical Data

It is found that exhibits "A" and "B" are both written with a nutgall ink. Both specimens show much disintegration of the ink and deposits of foreign matter. Exhibit "B," however, plainly shows dilution of the ink. In spots exhibit "B" shows retouching with a lead pencil. The apex of the down stroke of the capital "D" at the beginning of the message is in lead pencil. The "C" in the word "captured" on the same line has been retouched with pencil.

Writing Habits

I find the following writing habits consistent in all specimens. For instance, the habit of crossing the "t"s high or to the right or left of that letter; see

Exhibit "B" line 1, the word "captured," line 2, the words "something" and "everything," line 6, the words "notify" and "Qts"

Exhibit "C" line 3, "department" line 11, "disability" line 24, "to" line 26, "thanks"

The writer's habit of using capitals at the beginning of words in the middle of a sentence is significant. . . .

Exhibits "B" and "C" both show a ragged right-hand margin, even where there is room for the succeeding word . . . .

All specimens show alternating overhand and underhand writing. Note Exhibit "B" line 1, the word "burning" Exhibit "C," line 3, the "m" and "n" in "Department."

Similarities

Exhibit "B" lines 3 and 4, the terminal flourish on the word "crew"
Exhibit "A" line 16, the word "crew"
Exhibit "C" line 19, the word "threw"

. . .

The small "r"s in the message, in their varied forms are clearly reproduced in exhibits "A" and "C." Wherever the small "r"s are found at the end of a word, see Exhibit "B" line 4, the word "over" the "r" terminates with an upward hook bending to the left and ending with pressure. This characteristic is found repeated in Exhibit "C" line 12, the word "water," line 13, the word "tender."

. . .

The rolling style of writing adopted in Exhibit "B" for the purpose of disguise, is more or less normal to the writer and can readily be seen on the back of Exhibit "A" the words "letter" and "write."

In conclusion, it may be said that these writings are entirely consistent in shading, slant, form, pen pressure, and involuntary unconscious writing movement beyond the possibility of mere coincidence or the temporary acquisition by another person.

B. C. Farrar
Examiner in Questioned Handwriting

LULA WORMELL

57 Lawn Avenue
Portland, Maine
Late August 1921

If I had the strength, I would walk to the florist's and buy a wreath and then hire a taxicab to take me out to Cape Elizabeth so I might sling it into the sea. But my strength has failed me, and I cannot even do that one sad simple thing.

Mother learned last night of what you have done, Christopher Gray. She read it in the Boston newspaper, and then she told me. Reverend Lorimer wondered if this might be another Hearst papers' invention, but, coming from Mr. Richey as it did, I knew at once in my heart it was true.

You coward. You base, despicable, lying coward! And for four months now I had thought you my hero.

I only wish you were in Maine and had to face the both of us, to look into our eyes and hear not so much our low opinion of you, sir, but to hear our questions of you, a grown man, and one who has been a sailor in the United States Navy, yet. My father would've sized you up and had you told him you had more than ten years in the service, he likely would've said, "A Navy man is good enough for me. Get your gear and get aboard!"

Not good enough for *me*, though, Mr. Gray, not anymore. Father was kind, kind and generous to a fault—didn't he let that vicious mate McLellan step straight out of a Barbadian jail and back onto the *Deering*? This part of my father, this warmth and friendship everyone knew in him, I shall never live up to now, and I know that—his fate, and that of his ship, have left me bitter, I'm afraid.

And now atop that bitterness you have poured the purest gall I've ever known.

Tell me, Mr. Gray, how a man can live with himself, a man who can fabricate such a lie as you have, who can rekindle a brokenhearted family's hopes, who can even set the powers of his nation to work—all as if in good faith—to discover the truth about missing men and lost ships, while every bit of it was built upon falsity and deceit. How does such a man face the rising sun each morning?

Perhaps you don't—perhaps you are like some creature of the night, a man of stealth with cloak of darkness . . . ha! I am so furious at you that I am sitting here in Father's chair making you more than you are, hearing my mad brain spin words that, if I don't stop, will have you become something large and awful, like Milton's Lucifer. But you are not like that at all, Christopher Gray, this I know. There is nothing grand about you, not even the evil story you spun.

You, sir, are so petty, so small of mind that you will never know the full extent of the harm you have done. Oh, you well know what you have set in motion in my home, and in the government, and you may think it little enough that the wife and daughter of a man you will never meet have poured the fullest measure of their hearts and souls into this, and that the leaders of your nation have put every resource forward that they possibly could in pursuit of a will-o'-the-wisp your lie engendered. Having wasted so much of our spirits and gained nothing for yourself but dishonor, a badge you'll wear always, you probably have neither the forthcomingness nor imagination to comprehend, to appreciate fully what you have cost us, and what hurt you have inflicted upon people who had never bothered you in the least, or intended you any harm whatsoever.

I am so worn out and numb and feel so cruelly toward you that, for the first time in my life, I think I can comprehend what cruelty really is: not feeling, or caring about, the ruin it is causing even as it is doing so. An iron coldness in the blood that you must have and that thank God in heaven I do not!

In time I will recover that piece of my heart that now seems fallen away. I cannot cry, nor feel such antipathy as I do, for all time. Even if He hasn't yet, God will give me balm someday. And in spite of your perfidy and all the stock I put in it, knowing no better than I did and hope being—delusive though it is—so necessary to us all, I still believe Father is alive somewhere and that in time the worst, longest moment of my life will draw to a close.

You, though, Mr. Gray, will find that promise out of reach, for you have borne false witness. A few false markings of an ink pen upon a small piece of paper and you have floated your immortal soul out to sea and damned yourself by breaking one of God's own Ten Commandments.

Far more would I prefer to stand before God as a fool, but a faithful one, than to have him find me out as an evil deceiver. He who sees the least sparrow fall will have the time I pray to pass judgment on you, just enough time to send you straight to Satan, with whom you can lie for all eternity.

You stare at the same rising and setting sun that I do, the same moon, and you watch the same ocean in all its endless rolling, and you remember what I have said.

For I am done with you. Forever.

So be it, so help me God.

W. O. SAUNDERS

Offices of the Independent
505 East Fearing Street
Elizabeth City, North Carolina
Friday, September 2, 1921

Now we know. Now the whole world knows—Christopher
Columbus Gray of Buxton is a fake and a fraud. Why is it that we're furious, yet not surprised?

One insignificant and selfish little man feigns, and his feint, this
bottle note, sets the maritime world and the newspapers crazy. Alarms
the navy, lights a fire under the Justice Department, causes an investigative collaboration between the very secretary of commerce and the
secretary of state. Not a bad day's work, you might say, if you admire
folks who can conjure up something out of nothing and make some
good of it.

But I just wish somebody would tell me what good this man's lie has
done, and what good is this abject liar himself?

I am sorely tempted to walk down to Water Street wharf here this
coming Sunday and plunk my dollar seventy-five down and climb
aboard the *Annie Vansciver* and steam on down to Nags Head and go on
to Hatteras and see this fellow. Look into his face, and see for myself
how such a faker holds himself once the world knows him for what he
is. But to do that I'd surely miss the boat coming back that night, and
though my curiosity's something big, all right, I just don't think Mr.
Gray is worth it, after all.

So much for pastoral fantasy and noble savages—here in this man
Gray we have an *ignoble* savage, if ever there were such a beast. Anybody who thinks that all the confidence men congregate in cities, and
that our quiet countrysides are somehow innocent of such people, anyone so willfully credulous had best remember that at the heart of the
Garden of Eden lay a snake. Take a good look, from afar if you will, at
this scoundrel—no interloper he, but a man homegrown right down
there on Hatteras Island amongst the salts of the earth.

Even Hatteras—and I'm not speaking against Dare County, not for one single second. No one loves that beautiful, forlorn coast more than I do, and, if I live long enough, I swear I'll see a monument built to the Wright Brothers down there and I hope I'll see some playwright make of the lost colony's tale an American *Oberammergau*. Pardon me if a country editor takes a moment and dreams a dream. The thing about dreams, though, and I have to catch myself and remember this, is that every now and again one of them's going to be a nightmare, and mark my words what we've heard from Hatteras this season is enough to make a body believe he's wide awake and dreaming some pretty awful stuff.

A schooner founders, a crew vanishes. Mr. Duff's load of pianos sinks down there in the sound. Another schooner sails up and sits on the beach at Bodie Island, the *Laura Barnes*, scarcely six months old, and Bath-built, too, that ship. And not two weeks after the *Laura Barnes* comes in, Senator Simmons is holding forth about ocean freighters someday landing at Elizabeth City here—nobody ever exactly called Furnifold M. Simmons a visionary, but coming when they did, his remarks just sounded a little, well, *odd*.

And then here's young Leary in his shadboat sailing up from Hatteras in all his grief, bearing his mistress (having lived with her one scant year in a state of natural love on the farthest reach of that island!) a corpse up the Pasquotank to shroud and bury her here amongst the Episcopalians.

Tell me there's not something passing strange in *all* of this—and it didn't take any fake note in a bottle to make it so.

Passing strange!

A LETTER TO GARD DEERING
Baltimore, Maryland
September 6, 1921

Captain Richard Fick, master of the schooner *Lydia McL. Baxter*, a Deering ship, turned in to the FBI a letter addressed to Gardiner G. Deering, Bath, Maine, and dated August 26, 1921. The letter read:

Dear Sir:

Just send to notify you that you may have a captain in readiness to send for the Schr. *L. Mc. Baxter* the next time she sails if the law of the United States give Captains privilege to carry two guns to bluff men trying to make an honest living then men are at liberty to defend their selves. This get rich quick is driving that man crazy by trying to run out men and get their money. He and his wife should go to sea alone in the vessel and don't carry no one else to be dogs. We are not going to stand for it. The wages is down and we are willing to work for a little to make an honest living but not to be a dog. He is mate and his wife is captain. She pick every news she can to make trouble but we will cure it one of these days. They shall both run over board, so be in readiness.

Yours truly

Reds

The captain believed the letter to have been composed by a former mate of his, a man named Marcial who was at this time apparently living in Philadelphia, and he thought that Marcial could give good information about the mysterious schooner *Carroll A. Deering* and that maybe he had even been among her crew, for he had been heard to say:

"Some of the members of the *Deering*'s crew are now walking the streets of Philadelphia, Pennsylvania."

GUMSHOE IN PHILLY

Philadelphia, Pennsylvania
September 6, 1921

As soon as Agent Jenkins in Baltimore phoned Captain Fick's report northward, Agent Poling hit the Philly streets. Though he didn't find Marcial at the South Bancroft address Fick had given, he learned that Marcial had lived there until very recently and just moved a few days earlier to 1744 Lombard. There Poling got his man, and Martin Marcial, who had followed the sea for eighteen years, admitted that he knew Charles McLellan, the *Deering*'s first mate.

"Met him about two and a half years ago," said Marcial. "In New York, near the Seaman's Mission, at the offices of J. A. Hall, Shipping Master."

"You know him well?" asked Poling.

"I saw him and talked with him probably eight or ten times."

"Know where he was born?"

"No—I think he was from the West Indies, because he speaks like a British West Indian."

"Well, that's a start. How would you describe him?"

"Thirty-eight or forty years old, six feet, hundred and eighty pounds. Very dark complexion and a red mustache."

"Have you kept in touch with him?"

"Not since New York City."

"What about the crew from that schooner? You know anything about where they might be now?"

"Mr. Poling," Martin Marcial said, "I don't know anything about the *Carroll A. Deering* except what I've read in the newspaper."

"Not a thing?"

"Not a thing."

THE ITALIAN QUESTION

Royal Italian Embassy
1400 New Hampshire Avenue
Washington, D.C.
September 9, 1921

An Italian steamer, the *Monte San Michele*, left New York with a cargo of wheat on February 2, 1921, bound for Gibraltar and then for Italy. The *Monte San Michele* never made port, and now the Italian government wished to know what the American Bureau of Navigation had learned about the mysterious disappearances of so many ships.

The Italians had already been informed by the U.S. undersecretary of state that on February 8, 1921, the American steamer *Gasper* got a radiogram from the *Monte San Michele* requesting aid, her position then being latitude 36°N, longitude 49°40'W. When the *Gasper* had sailed to that position, she found not a trace of the troubled *Monte San Michele*.

Captain Civalleri of the Royal Italian Navy now took "the liberty of asking your Department whether it has concluded the inquiry begun for the purpose of discovering the cause of the mysterious disappearance of several American ships, and in the affirmative case, what are the results?"

OF MEN WITH LIKE NAMES

Pier 39
Galveston, Texas
January 4, 1922

Agent Sullivan of the FBI met the Danish steamship *Tranquebar*, just arrived at nine this morning, and took two of her sailors into custody: Peter Nilsen, a fireman, and H. C. Jensen, an able-bodied seaman. From the Texan docks the men went to the offices of the Danish consulate, 433 Security Building, where they were sworn and questioned by Sullivan.

Nilsen, born in Copenhagen in 1882, knew no English. In translation, he testified that from January to April 1921, he sailed aboard the Danish ship *Karen* between Denmark, England, and France. He had no idea where Cape Hatteras was, nor any notion whatsoever of the *Deering*.

Sullivan's second sailor—Hans Marten Charles Jensen, a twenty-five-year-old man from Karsoer, Denmark—spoke English well. Under oath, this Jensen allowed that he had been near Cape Hatteras only once, in 1919, on the bark *Elizabeth* sailing from Copenhagen to Hampton Roads, Virginia. He worked the docks of Odense, Denmark, during the months January through April 1921, and said simply,

"I never even heard of the schooner *Carroll A. Deering*."

Back to the *Tranquebar* the Danes were trundled, along with specific instructions for the captain of the unfortunate men whose names were just too similar to those of the lost *Deering* sailors:

"No shore leave or the usual liberties until further advised by the Danish Consul."

LULA WORMELL

57 Lawn Avenue
Portland, Maine
Late January 1922

What a long fall and, now, winter again already—nothing to show for any of it, and yet, still so many things that don't make sense.

Father had a roll of his own charts, five or six of them in a canvas cover four feet long, maybe five inches in diameter—there were many more charts than were sold at the public auction. All unaccounted for.

Astonishing, wasn't it, the Maine captain who claimed to've been actively interested in promoting the investigation then telling a gullible reporter that it was the opinion of seafaring people that the crew had left the *Deering* in her boats and been swamped.

In fact, this is in no sense true.

Six other captains from here around Portland have never changed their expressions—they all have always said this was never a case of ordinary shipwreck. These are men of the "old type" who sailed for many years for the same firm as Father—J. S. Winslow and Company— men who knew him well and knew how good his judgment was.

The wife of one of them came by in September—a woman who has been to sea for nearly thirty years and can herself navigate and manage ships—and said to me again how she and her husband thought the case was of a most unusual nature.

"Have you ever thought of intrigue?" she asked me. "Possibly foreign, carried on through Mexico."

Have we not?

Mr. Richey was kind enough to send the ocean chart to us, and some cards I'd mailed Father that someone retrieved from his desk—even a Kodak one of the FBI agents took of the remains of the *Deering* washed up on Ocracoke Island on the Carolina shore.

But that missing chart, the coastwise one, where is it? Father would've used this one from Cape Fear on—there is no reason why if the ocean chart were left there the other should not have been, if my father were in charge as usual. Someone somewhere knows much more about it all.

Somehow we have always felt that Mexico or Central America figures in this case and I still think so — there is a tangle or mystery yet unsolved. Where are our people? What can be done for them? I believe so very much they are alive!

Oh, it was most welcome news to receive Mr. Richey's letter of the 21st, to know he is still interested and ready to trace to the end any clue whatsoever. Rather a strange coincidence, and a gratifying one, too, that his letter came when it did, for this very week could not but be especially hard for us, as it is the one corresponding to the one of the mystery.

Fair weather, it was then, and the *Carroll A. Deering* was only a day or so from port.

Now I have this photograph of her remnants.

Now it has been a year. One solid, awful year.

Somehow, I do believe the Truth may yet be known.

RUMORS

Along the North Carolina coast
Late Spring 1922

"You know all these sub-chasers the navy's retired and sold off?"

"Sure."

"You know what's come of em, don't you?"

"I've heard talk, but talk's cheap."

"Yeah, that's right, but whiskey ain't, not in this day and age. Bootleggers've got em and they're usin' em like revenue cutters, their crews're all decked out in uniform, like real navy."

"You got to be kiddin' me — why the hell the bootleggers puttin' on a show for the Coast Guard? They gon fool the Coast Guard, try and slide by thataway?"

"I oughta quit talkin' to you, you idiot. You can't fool the Coast

Guard that easy—they hauled one of these decommissioned boats, *Navy 217* it was, over to Lookout Bight to check her out. She weren't a smuggler, but she might've been."

"Yeah, that's the talk I heard, bunch of boys carrying on about her out at the menhaden plant, over at Town Creek."

"Right. The ones the fake boats're tryin' to trick is the *other* damn *bootleggers*—the ones goin' from down in the West Indies on up to Philly and New York all full of booze. The subchasers catch em, shake em down, and then *they*'ve got the whiskey. One bunch of bootleggers stealing from the other, that's what's goin' on out there."

"Well, ain't that against the *law*?"

"You're a damn fool, is what you are."

LAST LETTERS

No one forgot.

The unknown, unfound kernel of such a mystery has always possessed the power to vex and amaze and intrigue souls from one generation to the next, on and on. Perhaps the only turn of spirit that can outlast abject human lamentation is the one that compels unceasing wonder, even as its spark and source fades and decays and turns once again into dust, the cascading questions always the same: What happened? What have we overlooked? What truth-telling matter of fact has been right before us all along, ours for thorough comprehension, but that we have not held up and examined, or beheld in the proper light?

No one gave up—certainly not the Reverend Doctor Addison B. Lorimer, the Wormell family's preacher back in Portland. On the 31st of March, 1922, Reverend Lorimer sat down and wrote Coast Guard Commandant William Edward Reynolds in Washington, asking to be furnished a statement about weather and surf, as reported by the light vessels off the Carolina capes for the last eight days of January 1921.

Commandant Reynolds replied on April 3 that those vessels were not under his jurisdiction, their responsibility and oversight belonging instead to the Department of Commerce, to which he referred the preacher's request with dispatch, sending it specifically to Lawrence Richey. "I fully appreciate," wrote Reynolds to the preacher in Maine, "your keen interest in clearing up the mystery surrounding the *Deering*."

On April 6, 1922, Mr. Richey requested from the Bureau of Lighthouses "reports covering the weather and sea conditions between the dates of January 23d and January 31st, 1921, inclusive, in the vicinity of Diamond Shoal, Cape Lookout Shoal, and Frying Pan Shoal Light Vessels," and in a little less than a month, the commissioner of lighthouses drafted a seven-line transmittal, stating, "I beg to inclose certified copies of the information desired, taken from the original deck logs of these light vessels." That was May Day 1922, and the commissioner's short note was entitled *Weather Reports. Memorandum for Secretary of Commerce*.

On the 8th of May, Lawrence Richey sent to Reverend Lorimer these detailed reports, for his and Mrs. Wormell's and Lula Wormell's perusal, drawing no conclusions and leaving these three folks in Maine to take the old jottings on wind and wave and gaze upon them as if the ciphers were near-mystic figures suspended within a bell glass, and to make of the old Carolina weather whatever in the world they could.

A TELEGRAM FROM SOUTH AMERICA

American Consul General
Valparaiso, Chile
September 14, 1922

TO THE HONORABLE THE SECRETARY OF STATE, WASHINGTON, D.C.: ABLE-BODIED SEAMAN ANSWERING THE NAME AND DESCRIPTION OF PETER SORENSEN IS NOW ON BOARD THE DANISH SHIP *KRONBORG*, WHICH SAILED FROM VALPARAISO FOR NEW YORK CITY SEPTEMBER 13TH.

MEET THE *KRONBORG*

Department of State
Washington, D.C.
September 14, 1922

Thirteen months had passed since Lawrence Richey exposed Christopher Columbus Gray's manuscript in a bottle as fraudulent, when a slender lead in the *Deering* case surfaced in Valparaiso. The third assistant secretary of state, upon receipt of the Chilean telegram, informed the Bureau of Navigation:

"I have asked the Attorney General to have this man examined upon arrival in New York in order to ascertain whether or not he was on board the *Carroll A. Deering* at the time of its loss."

Did FBI men collar Peter Sorensen after the Danish ship *Kronborg* ended her sail from Valparaiso and on through the Panama Canal and up the American east coast and finally made port in New York, and, if so, was this Sorensen the twenty-nine-year-old seaman who reportedly sailed with the *Frederiksborg* in early 1922, or the *same* nineteen-year-old able-bodied seaman Peter Sorensen who had sailed on the *Deering*'s last voyage? Or yet another man, merely with like name?

Beyond these brief communications, the record, alas, went silent.

FILING THE CLAIM

New York, New York
October 30, 1922

The last card thrown down upon the table of this sad game was another letter, a real one this time, written in dead earnest and quite far away from either the shoals of Carolina or the rocky coast of Maine. Its author was an insurance firm's attorney, and shadowing his one-page correspondence to the federal government seeking certification for the family's insurance claim was Lula Wormell's matter-of-fact admission of defeat, heartbreak, and loss. She was still positive that something well out of the ordinary, some foul play or bizarre happenstance, had befallen her father, but she was by now just as secure in the awful knowledge that she would never see him again in this world.

New York, Oct. 30, 1922
Policy No. 644,589—Willis B. Wormell

Coast Guard
Treasury Department,
Washington, D. C.

Gentlemen:

We are advised that the five-masted schooner *Carroll A. Deering*, owned by the G. G. Deering Company of Bath, Maine, left Barbados for Norfolk, Virginia, January 9, 1921. We are advised that the chart of the schooner which is in the possession of the Government shows that Captain Willis B. Wormell was on the said vessel when it was off Cape Fear, Sunday, January 23, 1921. We are further advised that the following Sunday night the vessel went on the Outer Diamond Shoal off Cape Hatteras. Nothing further was ever heard of the vessel or any member of its crew. We are writing you for the purpose of asking if you will kindly furnish us with a certificate showing that the records of the Government show that the said vessel has been reported as wrecked or missing and further setting forth that the said Captain Wormell was on board the vessel at the time that it was lost, and that he is dead.

Very truly yours,
Frederick L. Allen
General Solicitor
The Mutual Life Insurance Company of New York

And so with these few unemotional words, uttered for them by another, Lula Wormell and her mother gave up a father and a husband for dead and asked people they did not know for whatever monies there might be coming to them from the policy insuring the life of one Willis B. Wormell, ship's captain, late of the *Carroll A. Deering*.

THE COMMANDANT'S REPLY

U.S. Coast Guard Headquarters
Washington, D.C.
November 9, 1922

A week and a half later, O. M. Moore, acting commandant of
the Coast Guard, replied to lawyer Allen, citing the "casualty report on
file in this office furnished by G. G. Deering Company, Bath, Maine,
owners," which declared the vessel "a total loss" and stated that "the
fate of whom [the crew] was unknown." Commandant Moore further
quoted a letter that accompanied the Deering report: "The *Deering* put
into Lewes, Del., Sept. 2, Capt. Merritt sick, and Capt. W. B. Wormell,
of Portland, Maine, was sent on to relieve him, which he did."

Which he did.

LULA WORMELL

57 Lawn Avenue
Portland, Maine
Late 1922

"The ocean is your friend," Father always said, "if you let it be."

"What does that mean, though?" I used to ask him.

"Well," he answered, "you can't fight it. Oh, you can, but you
can't fight it and expect to win."

"Fight it how?" I'd ask. I was just a little girl then, the first time I
heard him say this. He spoke quickly, as if he were nervous about getting what he had to say said, as if he had too many things to say and not
quite enough time. Yet, though he spoke and moved in a quick fashion,
there was behind it a calm, a surety about himself, and I trusted him
and believed in him as if he were the greatest rock the coast of Maine
had ever known.

We were down at the seashore, and he was teaching me to swim. He
had a great fear for sailors, fishermen, or for any people who spent any
part of their lives upon the water, or in towns and villages beside it, who
didn't know how to swim and never took time to learn. It was almost

like asking to die, he said once, but that was later—Father would never have said such a frightening thing to me when I was small. Just that it mystified him, because he knew that everyone working and living around the water would be in it somehow, sometime. And then what? God made men, and men made boats, and God also made, it seems like, a thousand ways for men to fall out of boats. Or to be pitched out, tossed out, blown or thrown out. A man who couldn't swim would drown in a minute, but a man who could at least had a chance.

And so did a woman who could, and he would see to it that I would be one of those. Even if Mother feared it for me just as she feared it for herself.

"The ocean is your friend," he would say, and there we were in the cove at Harpswell, I floating on my back, he standing over me with one hand beneath the back of my head, the other at the small of my back, keeping me up and letting me feel my own buoyancy and get used to it, and trust it as I trusted him. Never more than a few minutes, just a little, just enough. Somehow he knew when to take me back into the shallows and let me play there on the beach. And then, later, he began to turn me over, his arms like a cradle under me, so I could kick and work my arms and breathe, always breathe, not gasp for air or gulp it, just take it in easy.

"But fight it *how*?" I wanted to know.

He took me up all in his arms—how old was I? eight?—and got me round on his back, then sank into the sea, till only his head was above water. Landward we faced, and he said, "The sea when it looks angry *is* angry—"

"Angry at what, Father?"

"I don't know, Lula, only God does. Angry at itself, perhaps. At us for being out upon it in ships when perhaps we shouldn't be, or maybe at the sky, just for being above it. But you know what an angry ocean looks like, don't you, Lula?"

"Yes, I think so."

"All tossing and spuming and fuming, spray everywhere, breakers and foam, not one thing *still* about it."

"Yes."

"God has made it easy for us to know that anger, easy for us to see it, to steer clear of it, or, better yet, if we are fortunate, not to be out and about in it, not to be steering at all."

"And stay at home?"

"And stay at home if you're a captain and you can—or put into the nearest harbor of refuge and wait it out, though it may mean days in port, and no headway and time lost to the shipper. But that is the way of it. And there is another anger the ocean can have about it, not one so easily seen as the storm-tossed seas. Some days, for some reasons none of us yet know, the pull of the undertow is much greater than it usually is, and that is not something you can see at a glance. Or riptides may be at play, and the line at the surface where two great underwater forces meet may be hard for your eyes to perceive and yet you find yourself in it and going quickly seaward . . ."

The forenoon sun was so bright, the slack sea so blue, it almost hurt to keep my eyes open, and Father was so particular, the way he was talking. The troubled sea, though nothing like the water in which we were just then immersed, was nonetheless so real.

"And then what, Father?"

"You will want to swim to the land, straight in, but you must not."

"Why?"

"If you do, you will be carried seaward, and you may drown. This is what I meant—you cannot fight it. If you swim to the side, though, the sea will free you, for the riptides, though strong, are also narrow. And once you are free from the grip of that tide, you will know, you will feel it, and then and only then can you swim straight for the shore again."

"The ocean is your friend," I said, trying Father's words as my own now, as if I had heard and known them forever.

"*If,*" he said, "*if* you let it be."

In Down East Maine the sea is blue and cold, as I have heard it is in North Carolina. Father has followed and loved the sea all his days, and out of love respected her—if ever a man let the ocean be his friend, it was he. So why, then, friend of mine, did it take Father's ship six days to travel a mere eighty miles? And whose hand took over from Father's and marked the ocean chart after his ship reached Frying Pan?

And where, friend, is he now?

It is awful how much I am now become like the girl in that old folk-song, the one who stands on the ocean's shore before the sea, asking the sea what has become of her sailor boy, asking the sea to take the rose she places on the crest of a wave and let it rest upon his watery grave, but to every question she asks each chorus of the song always answers the same—

O, what does the deep sea say?
What does the deep sea say?
It moans and groans and splashes and foams
And rolls on its weary way.

W. O. SAUNDERS
Offices of the Independent
505 East Fearing Street
Elizabeth City, North Carolina
Late 1922

Every time I think I've done enough puzzling over things in my life, something like this schooner *Carroll A. Deering* fetches up and presents itself, and I've got to start puzzling and figuring and ciphering all over again. I don't know why these mysteries seem to keep seeking us out and landing on our geographic doorstep, on our very shores, but they do. When you think about it, here's a part of the world where the very first thing that happened to it—that we know much about, anyway—was the colony disappeared.

Our first colony was a lost colony. Maybe that ought to've told us something.

I've got a newspaper to put out, for God's sakes, so I don't know why, either, that I spend seems like half my time messing with stuff like this.

But it's hard to think about one thing without tying it in with another, and the *Deering* with its vanished crew, that sets me in mind of Theodosia Burr—you know about her, don't you? Aaron Burr's daughter, married to the governor of South Carolina, sailing north to see her father in New York City, and her ship, the *Patriot*, never made that port. What it did do was float in to the seabeach at Nag's Head, sails set, rudder lashed, and the Outer Bankers boarded her, found her deserted and without charts or papers, and claimed it for themselves, as was their fashion. One of the men who rowed out to her and boarded her was John Tillett, and he salvaged an oil portrait of a beautiful woman, gave it to his wife and after he died she married a Mann, as in Mann's Harbor, and then Dr. Pool from here in Elizabeth City, *he* got that painting years later from her—he was one of the summerfolk and she was old Polly Mann living back in Nag's Head Woods—when she paid him with it for a house call and different ones saw it here in Betsy Town and after quite a while it turned out it was Theodosia and that's how they knew it was her ship. A hundred and some years ago, let me see, I've got a file on it here somewhere—yes, 1812, December 1812, and Dr. Pool got the picture just after the Civil War, in 1869.

So here it is 1921 and I can't believe it's been thirteen years since I started up this newspaper, the *Independent*, in Elizabeth City, and the whole reason I'm here more than somewhere, anywhere, else, that, too, is on account of a mystery—Nell Cropsey who disappeared that's twenty years ago now, and Jim Wilcox who did time for killing her, now he's back here, been back three years already.

I've got files on all this—that's what a newsman does, after all—keep files.

The *Deering* now—from what we know . . . well, that's one thing, and what we actually know is precious little. You change a pair of words, though, just a couple, and then we're off into thinking about *for all we know*.

For all we know, the captain died during that hurricane offshore—they say you see his hand on the ocean chart only up to January 23rd—and they buried him at sea and that's why he didn't do the hailing when the *Deering* passed the lightship at Lookout Shoals. Except the crew wanted a report made back to the ship's owners about lost anchors and chains from the storm, so why wouldn't they've reported a dead captain, too? Maybe he was hurt during the storm, was hurt and laying up in his cabin and couldn't come to the rail and do the hailing himself. That would've been less of something to report, I figure.

And as for the hailer having a foreign accent? Well, the mate, Mc-Lellan, he was a Scot, wasn't he? And the bos'n, Frederickson, was a Swede or a Finn, depending on who you believe. Now I know a Scot and a Swede or Finn, whichever one he really was, they aren't going to sound anything alike, but either way, either one's going to sound good and foreign shouting across water at some distance. You take your favorite Irishman or Hungarian, what have you, and go on out to the big-sea water and have a conversation boat to boat and try and tell them apart, tell what kind of foreign it is that's coming at you.

For all we know, though, First Mate McLellan had made a side-deal, maybe had some of that Scandinavian crew in it with him, while they were down there raising hell in Barbados, and maybe, just maybe, had a bunch of Barbadian rum stashed in the *Deering* somewhere. Plenty of room—that's a big ship, after all, and she was coming back light. No, it's not the most brilliant of plans, but this is Prohibition, and that real rum'd be worth a whale of a lot more around Norfolk than all this East Lake white liquor—they don't call it popskull for nothing, drinking men tell me—coming up over the sound, through here, flowing north to the navy.

Anyhow, as far as the West Indies smuggling goes, there was a case just a few months after the *Deering* foundered, in August of '21, the Coast Guard picked up a two-masted British schooner at Ocracoke Inlet—the *Messenger of Peace*. Bound from Nassau to Jacksonville, not the one in North Carolina but Florida. A mite out of the way, I'd say, and so would anybody else with good sense. Her crewmen said they'd run out of water and were looking to get some at Ocracoke. Coast Guard let this so-called *Messenger of Peace* go, suspicious of her though they were, but they had occasion soon enough to pick her up again off Ocracoke, end of December '21—this time she said she was bound from Nassau to Nova Scotia, and again she was out of drinking water but now, mind, she was also out of food and fuel. And the Caribbean crewmen were freezing. And she was taking on seawater. Her cargo the Coast Guard reported as "assorted liquor"—I reckon so, *two thousand cases* of it!—and they had the cutter *Seminole* tow the *Messenger* on down to Wilmington till they could sort it all out. Moored her at the customhouse, inside of which they stored the contraband—and then two men got caught trying to bust in after the whiskey, while the *Messenger* nearly sank in the Cape Fear at her moorings!

Back in July '21, the Prohibition boss Roy Haynes up in Washington had said they were going to have a big, old-fashioned dragnet off the Carolina coast, using both the Coast Guard *and* the navy. I know that made old Furnifold Simmons happy, and I guess the *Messenger* was one of their catches.

But the *Deering* boys, how would they've pulled it off? I don't know— but this was before the dragnet, and our coast has always been famously underpatrolled. If those sailors were already in serious trouble with the *Deering*'s captain, or over his already sealed fate, why mightn't they load their contraband onto the ship's boats and make a run at Hatteras Inlet? That's assuming that at least one man Jack amongst them had a pretty good idea of the inside waters. One thing's sure: if they were loaded with liquor they had plenty to deal.

An inlet, the old salts say, is a tricky thing by day, when you can see the shape and size and color of the water, how much of it's breaking and gone white, and I've heard maritime men here in Elizabeth City say out of respect that even the Lord God, if he were trying to cross the bar at night and sail through Ocracoke or Hatteras Inlet in the dark, would say His prayers first before He did.

So maybe they sailed not away from Diamond Shoals, but *for* them, because they had Hatteras Light to lead them in. And they abandoned the *Deering* that evening, this is Sunday the 30th of January now, in the dark, the seas being smooth, and tried to bring the two ship's boats in through Hatteras Inlet. What they don't figure on is the wind picking up, because it's been light all day that Sunday. But it shifts around from the northwest to the southwest and picks up after dark and by midnight it's blowing fifteen to twenty and it's breezing up all night and all the next day and they're overloaded and they go down well before they're anywhere near the inlet with those two boats and with a west wind and then a north wind most of that Monday, the 31st, they're swept way away well out to sea and no one's the wiser about this mischief, or any other.

For all we know.

LULA WORMELL

57 Lawn Avenue
Portland, Maine
Late 1922

How I regret the things we never did, Mother and I. All wrapped up here on Lawn Avenue in the cold comfort of home without Father.

Oh, I'm a most practical woman about it all, I tell you. A port is not a port all by itself—not lest people come and go. We all know that. And that is the bargain, the arrangement, the marriage, if you will, of a town on the edge and its stores and its goods—and the river or the sea that laps at it.

Why isn't it some comfort to me to state the pattern, to review the compact?

Never a goodbye.

Never a kiss.

Never anymore his quick entry and firm stand at the hallway door and his arms out almost from sidelight to sidelight and his "Did you miss me, Lula?" Never.

You don't think the *never* at the time, the last time you see them. You just think they'll be back because they always are, they always have been. This is the way, the *only* way, captains and their wives, their daughters, their women, have managed all down through time. It cannot be any other way. "Well, there you go, then" and "Now, here you are back again." We know any time can be the last time, yet we refuse it always.

We say no to death.

Now, I want to tell about our church, our big rock Central Square Baptist Church, only a little ways from our home here on Lawn Avenue. This is where his coffin would have lain, where his funeral would've been, had we ever found him.

An unmarked death, an unrelieved mourning—what an awful crime against our kind. Not something we wish upon ourselves, but that which is forced upon us by circumstance.

My father was the best—

Did he give up the ship at Tuckernuck Shoal in '14?—of course not. And in '21, why, the best schoonerman in America would not have driven his ship upon the worst shoals in America—you can count on that! And even *if he had*, he would've stayed with the ship because that is what he knew to do and that is what we *know* him to have done with the *Alice M. Lawrence*—how much plainer can it be?

All the sea captains agree—you know what Captain Holden said, master of the schooner *Josephine McQuestion*? He called Father "one of the best masters that ever sailed a schooner, far too wise a sailor to get off the ship and take chances with the breakers on shore."

Oh, yes, I'm a practical miss, I am—and what am I left with, when I sift through things like this? Simply that my father Captain Wormell was missing, subdued, dying, or dead when person or persons unknown hailed the Lookout Light Vessel, *certainly* by the time the *Deering* sailed diagonally across the shipping lanes in opposition to all he knew and to all he could have easily observed, were he alive and well.

My father did not ground that schooner. My father did not direct the last end of that ship and her crew.

I miss you so very, very much, my poor, lost father. Daddy. Dads. I love you, and may you sail forever and always in my heart, always safe passage, always safe home.

Always, Captain.

A BOS'N SPEAKS

Elizabeth City, North Carolina
February 1939

Keith Saunders, son of the *Independent* editor W. O. Saunders, was doing a story on the *Deering* for the *State* magazine up in Raleigh, and he got to talking with Chief Boatswain Charles O. Peele, U.S. Coast Guard, Seventh District headquarters. Peele had been a surfman stationed at Creeds Hill on the Outer Banks in 1921, and he claimed he was a surfman in the first boarding party that first got onto the *Deering* eighteen years before.

"What happened to the crew of the *Deering* never was a mystery to me," said Bos'n Peele. "There were davits near the starboard rail, a little forward of midship, indicating that the schooner had carried a launch or lifeboat of some description, but no such boat was to be found. It is my opinion, that the seven men on board the schooner, realizing that she was stuck fast on the shoal, put their lifeboat or launch over and made for shore, but were swamped in the treacherous waters that swirl around Outer Diamond Shoals, and went to a watery grave. The fact that neither the boat nor the bodies of any of the men ever washed ashore is no puzzle at all, because there has never been a known instance where the body of a man drowned on Outer Diamond Shoals washed up on the beach.

"The schooner had undoubtedly carried some small boat, and that boat was missing. And it is very easy to see how the boat could have been swamped in trying to cross Outer Diamond Shoals, for that is one of the most dangerous and most treacherous spots known to maritime men on the Atlantic coast. In fact, those men would have been extremely lucky if they had made it across the shoals without capsizing. That, in my opinion, is what happened to the crew of the *Deering*, and I can't see why it was ever considered much of a mystery."

"Why," asked Keith Saunders, "didn't you put this forward when all the official investigations were going on?"

"I did," said Peele, "but no one paid any attention to my theory. I reckon that was because it was so plausible. They were all too busy at that time, tracking down all sorts of wild theories, and chasing wild geese."

CARROLL A. DEERING

Bay Point, Maine

August 11, 1940

He was what one would call a home fellow.

Truth to tell, he was a timid man and always had been, and had long known it, too. A young boy whom he taught how to drive remembered how Mr. Deering hated to be alone, how he would ask the boy to stay over in the house with him when his wife was away visiting kin. Yet he loved the water, loved to watch it any season, all the time, to watch the ships and small craft alike coming and going—he just would never have gone to sea, anymore than he'd cut his own arm off.

People thought it strange, perhaps, that a man whose father built ships never once shipped out himself.

And maybe they thought it odd as well that such a man spent his time building model ships, but that is what he did. *Endeavor*, from 1768. The battleship *Maine*—remember the *Maine*, you know. *Olympia*, she was Admiral Dewey's flagship. A New York City fireboat, supposed to be the biggest one in the world.

Yes, he was the Deering who stayed home. His brother Harry, now, he was off to sea a few times, but always as a passenger, never signed on as crew. They worked together in the shipyard office, G. G. Deering Company, and their brother Frank was foreman of the yard. Carroll Deering never went out on the bounding main, yet the ocean sea was within him all the same, and he could muse:

Ninety-nine ships the old man put to sea, and the very last one he named for me.

The last one for me. And you know what happened to her on Diamond Shoals.

This old sailing pennant here's about all that's left of her. Oh, we got the bell off her, sure, a few things—not all that much, though, off a ship that'd just about fill up a football field! We'll unfurl the pennant outside the cottage here in a little bit, my daughter Elizabeth and I, and show you how big it is—though anyone who ever saw her knows it didn't look so awful big when it was flying from the top of *Deering*'s jig-germast.

And we'll see how it still catches the wind—yes, see the last of the wind catching the *Carroll A. Deering*.

LULA WORMELL CABANA

29 Vernon Place
Buffalo, New York
Early May 1948

Nearly thirty years have passed, though it hardly seems so, and almost all of thirteen since I married Leon Cabana.

Yes, I will see you, Mr. Snow.

Yes, you may come and speak with me in Buffalo.

Yes, I will tell you what I thought, what I believed, what I knew.

Hoover himself once listened to me, made a national mission out of my work and my strength and my good faith through it all. From me, Mr. Snow, you will hear the truth, see the ocean chart, as God is my witness . . . and my father's.

The truth is, I know Father was dead when the *Carroll A. Deering* foundered upon Diamond Shoals.

Why else were the sails all set instead of furled?

Why else was he not aboard, staying with the ship, trying to swing her off the shoals and save her or at least await rescuers and salvors as he had with the *Alice Lawrence*?

Why else was the ocean chart left behind and the coastwise chart taken? Whoever took over the marking of the *Deering*'s positions that last week could only have taken over from Father, and whichever man that was had something to hide.

Why else was the ship's large clock gone from the dining room?

Why else would Father himself not have hailed the master of the Cape Lookout lightship? And why else would the foreign mate (probably of Scottish birth) report lost anchors but *not* report my dead or dying father at that point?

Why else would they all be lounging about the quarterdeck like a host of drunkards unless that is what they were? Father alive and well would never have allowed it—he once fetched my cousin, who was shipping out with him, from the Portland train station and my cousin said the first greeting he got from my father was a kick in the seat of his pants and Father saying, "That's for nothing—now get aboard." Father was kind, but he was the master, too, and he made certain his seamen knew it even if it meant some demonstration and language. He'd not have lain idly by and let anyone else do the hailing, not unless he were dreadful sick, or dead.

They were coming from Barbados, for heaven's sake! That island was all afloat and awash in rum, and who knows but they smuggled a few barrels aboard to bring back in at Norfolk and the captain caught them at their game and the guilty ones turned on him.

Why else were things the way they were, and how else do they make any sense?

You come and visit with me, Mr. Snow, and we will speak slowly about it, for there are a good many details to this.

I know them each and every one by heart.

"HUNGRY BILL" MERRITT'S STATEMENT
21 Day Street
South Portland, Maine
May 12, 1948

Having called upon Lula Wormell Cabana in upstate New York, the Massachusetts nautical writer Edward Rowe Snow then traveled to Maine, where first he tracked down the *Deering*'s original captain and deposed him, with Captain Merritt stating:

I am now eighty-one years of age. I became ill at Delaware Breakwater, and Captain Wormell took my place. There were eleven men in the crew. I don't remember any red-headed man in the group. The engineer's name was Mr. Bates, and he was a reliable man. I believe that he put the note in the bottle, for it seemed to look like his writing. My solution is that the *Deering* ran ashore and the crew left the schooner. The small boat foundered in the breakers. Of course they might have murdered Captain Wormell, and again, they might not have.

It is so hard to prove anything that happens at sea—it is really a case where you've just got to guess at it.

CARROLL A. DEERING
398 Washington Street
Bath, Maine
June 1948

In the barn behind his home, Carroll A. Deering had mounted the *Deering*'s bell, salvaged from the schooner in February 1921. When Snow visited him, Deering took the writer out to the barn and showed him the bell, threw the barn doors open and struck it several times and let it peal out over the Kennebec River.

Then, at the old G. G. Deering shipyard on down Washington Street, long since closed and buildings shuttered and out of commission, Deering gave Snow a glimpse of one of the doomed schooner's riding lights, now stashed in a loft. A tiny office building held photographs and faded newspaper clippings, dusty mementos of his namesake vessel. The two men strode to the spot from which the *Deering* had been launched so long ago, then retraced their steps back to the office, where they sat and mulled the old case.

"What do you think happened to the *Deering*?" the shipbuilder's son at last asked his visitor.

Used to being the interrogator, Snow felt on the defensive, but he spun the yarn as best he could, recounting the known facts—Wormell's difficulty with the men in his crew all during the last voyage and the apparent absence of Wormell as a functioning captain during the final week of the ship's life (evidence of this being the other man's hand marking the chart, the strange figure hailing the lightship, the lounging crew on the quarterdeck)—and concluding that, at the end, someone else had his hand on the wheel and was running the ship.

"Probably the mate," Snow suggested.

Then he speculated that the mate may have killed Wormell, or that the true captain was injured or ill and, either way, was bedridden. Were the captain dead, and the crew spooked by the heavy weather they'd endured between Frying Pan and Lookout Shoals, abandoning ship and leaving her to drift and taking to the ship's boats once the seas went slack might have seemed their best way out. Maybe the steamer *Hewitt* picked them up, maybe not—since the *Hewitt*, too, was lost, no one could ever know. Maybe they were cast away and drowned with no witnesses save themselves.

Or, Snow carried on, the bootleg liquor trade might've been the cause of the *Deering*'s ruin, with rumrunners having taken over the vessel from the real crew, but in such a way they had quickly run her aground. To whatever extent the crew might've been involved, everyone—along with what contraband they had—fled the wreck in the boats in the dark, and the surf of Diamond Shoals finished them.

What did Carroll A. Deering make of all the palaver, all the conjecturing that day? If it worried him or unsettled him at all, any such effects must have been short lived, for Carroll Deering welcomed Snow for friendly visits in his home over the next decade. Snow would bring to Bath oddities of his own, old pistols once, another time a mahogany box, a cube of about a foot a side that caught the eye of Deering's grandson. Perhaps Snow appeared with his booty to repay Deering somehow for letting him in on what the Deerings knew of the old wrecked schooner, for showing him the ship's bell, and for ringing it loudly there in the village of the greatest of all sailing ships.

In time the *Deering*'s bell would pass on to the grandson, who as a man fished for a spell out of Hampton, Virginia, and then lived in Florida, a mariner himself, the master of supply boats and dive boats and small freighters. In time the man from Maine would know the lay of the Carolina sounds, and of her coast, and would reflect wryly on the shoalwater territory where his grandfather's namesake, the *Carroll A. Deering*, sailed to her end:

"A lot of water up there," he would say, "it's just kind of thinly spread."

But, before all that, he was once just a boy staring at a dark, mysterious box and wondering what lay within and hearing Mr. Snow ask Carroll Deering if he happened to have a bottle of wine handy. When Deering came forth with one, Snow opened the box wherein was a haunting vessel lined with silver, and the two older men and the boy then drank wine out of Snow's strange treasure—the skull, so he said, of Blackbeard the Pirate.

LULA WORMELL CABANA
29 Vernon Place
Buffalo, New York
June 1948

Being with Mr. Snow has brought it all back—all of it—and now I can't stop thinking about how much I hated to leave Portland, our home.

Yet I did not mind leaving Portland the city, the beginning of the trail to the sea, at all.

One fall evening, before I moved to Buffalo for good, I left the house and walked from Lawn Avenue, walked without thinking or even knowing where I was going and couldn't stop walking and didn't care if my highbutton shoes weren't made to walk miles, so I did—down the cobblestone alleys to the Fore River, and just stood awhile watching the harbor life as scant curtains of fog came gliding in and it got dusky dark and the lights came on all along the wharves down the way. All those big piers I knew as well as well! The Casco Bay Lines and the Custom House Wharf, the Chandler's Wharf and Union Wharf, yes, and the fish pier and market and all its sad, lingering smell of the sea, Mr. Wright's wharf, and Mr. Hobson's.

Oh, how I leaned on the seawall rail and loved every stick and timber of those old wharves and thought of a thousand times when Father and I went walking out to the river's end to see the whole length of some ship or another and how I'd always believed he'd let me sail with him someday—and though he never said *yes*, he never said *no* either—but that day never came, did it? And now never will, and I felt I was so heavy I could crush that railing down into the seawall, and the seawall down into the very river itself.

No one ever teaches us in school or church what to do when we meet our own ghosts, when we see our parents and ourselves, younger, with them, how we are to behave around them and what we are to say, or *not say*, to them. A moment later I felt so light I might've walked upon the autumn air across the Fore River and back again, stridden right into the shade of my old self and clasped Father's hand and gone into the fish market and gotten our dinner—*What'll it be, Miss Wormell, haddock or cod tonight?* Or, were it his ship among the forest of masts and rigging, just gone on and followed him up the gangplank and just sailed away even if it were to oblivion.

But oblivion, as the good Dr. Browne once said, is not to be hired. Father may have found it, though I would have had it otherwise, Lord knows. But that was not to be my fate.

Mine, now, was far from Portland, was here on other waters, those of Erie and Niagara. I had looked out upon my living past and seen myself separate from it, and as best I could made my peace with it and watched my father and my own girlhood vanish together on the Fore River's darkening wharves, and then blew it all a kiss farewell and turned and walked away, spent, toward home.

So I left all this, nearly thirty years ago, but all this did not leave me. If there *is* oblivion, it is not to be found, either, in this woman's breast, for I will always know myself as one thing and one thing only:

The captain's daughter.

EPILOGUE

What remained of the *Deering*'s bow, her capstan and skeletal frame, had long lain half buried on the seabeach of Ocracoke, washed over for decades by surf both mild and pounding, this section having drifted west-southwest from Diamond Shoals after the *Deering* broke up, even before the *Seminole* dynamited the back end of the wreck as a derelict and an endangerment to coastal waters and navigation. And here it settled and lay.

Until Hurricane Ione.

One of a hurricane triune—Connie and Diane being the other two—that drenched and devastated coastal Carolina with nearly fifty inches of rain during the Indian Summer of 1955, Ione blew through at dawn with hundred-mile-an-hour winds and freed the ghost ship from Ocracoke and set this partial *Deering* adrift again, northward now across the inlet to Hatteras Island, near Gooseville, where the tides of the passing storm left it.

Before long a Hatterasman named Wheeler Ballance appeared at the shore and in late October hauled the capstan and what timbers he could off to his filling station on the new all-paved highway into the village, a great schooner's last scraps now become derelict decor, all that remained of a ship that, once joined and mighty, was now shrinking away like the words *curiosity curious curio* till at long last *cure.*

ONE LAST LOOK

Buxton Woods
Cape Hatteras, North Carolina
April 9, 1969

An older woman drove her car through the live-oak forest of Buxton Woods, down along the nature trail south of Hatteras Light and past the campground there. She parked and walked southward, shuffling, stumbling across the dunes, fighting sandspurs, till at last she stood upon the last sand dune before Africa and for a long time stared seaward at the springtime ocean breaking over Diamond Shoals. The sandy strand was nothing at all like the rocky beach she knew back home in Harpswell, Maine, but the vast waters before her were the same great Atlantic she certainly did know that gave and took and took and gave and that would go on giving and taking till there was no longer any sea nor salt in it nor any more time either with which to ponder and take measure of it all.

The woman was Miriam Stover, the long-ago companion of Lula Wormell, who as a young woman had let Captain Wormell into her home so that he might turn in his cottage keys to her father before he took his vacationing family back into Portland, so he himself could train south to Delaware to take over the captaincy of the *Carroll A. Deering*. She wanted to see where the good captain may have met his end, and, too, where the very last of the grand Deering schooners had certainly met hers. If there were conch shells that could conjure for distant listeners the roar of the sea, then perhaps over the shoals the roaring sea itself, the very ocean at this very place, might whisper or cry or moan to her some clue to the mystery whose solution, whose answer seemed so achingly close she felt she could almost see it right there in the roiling surf.

Diamond Shoals went stretching out as far as her eyes could take it in, and then without saying it—for there truly was no one to say it to— she suddenly apprehended the overwhelming whole of it as a place of ruin, forlorn and far away from anything that tied her to the web of

Bow section and capstan of the *Carroll A. Deering* on the beach at Ocracoke Island, N.C.

earth, and she raised her camera, to capture and quell its foreign spirit, only to realize instantly that within it there was no film.

What the hell do I think I'm doing? she thought. At my age—old woman scrambling over sand dunes—to take pictures . . . of what? Bet I'd make a pretty picture. Out here in Hatteras nowhere but, God, this is where it was.

So what do I see here? What am I supposed to see? How do I gauge or judge this? There's nothing here! Nobody here to tell you where the ship sat out on those shoals. . . . I'd like to take a picture of the right ones, not just any shoals. Well, after all these years, what did I expect?

Nearly an hour she stood out upon the Buxton dune near Cape Point trying to penetrate a moment in time—a few hours at most—from nearly a half a century earlier. Finally she turned and walked through sea oats bending in the spring wind, then stumbled as if she had been pushed, regained herself and hurried, recoiling now from the demanding, pounding surf, running now, turning and nearly spraining her ankles in the sand, till at last she dismounted the rise and got to where the park service had grassed the sand and there was something like earth a lady from the firm and rocky coast of Maine could stand on.

Then Miriam Stover started and steered her car a few miles more down the island's strand to Hatteras village, where in front of Ballance's Texaco sat the capstan and a few timbers from the *Carroll A. Deering*. Kinsman of a onetime keeper of Hatteras Light, Wheeler Ballance had brought these shipwreck souvenirs to his station believing such an attraction might help his trade increase.

And so it did.

Miriam Stover tried to photograph the ship's pieces, but, working with a borrowed camera as she was, she had now somehow loaded the film backward. Back inside the filling station a tall man stepped forward to help her, and he asked her, though he already knew full well the answer, "What are you taking a picture of?"

"The remains of the *Carroll A. Deering*," Miriam Stover said.

"That so," the man said, then told her his tale. "My father, William Homan Gaskins Sr., was a member of the crew of the Coast Guard Cutter *Manning*. Her crew was the first to board the *Deering*. Several attempts had been made for four days to reach her, but the sea was so rough it was impossible. She had pounded so long on the shoals that her seams had opened when the *Manning* finally got to her. The Coast Guard took off what they could, and three weeks later after a severe storm they dynamited her as a menace to navigation. Queer thing, she was under full sail when she grounded, with food on the table, coffee in the pot, but tenders cut loose. No bodies ever washed up."

Nor will any, she thought. And she went forth from the little station and made from all different angles her pictures of the wood that may

Tourist lure, Hatteras Island, N.C.

well have grown to maturity not so very far from where she stood, and, once grown, been logged out of the coastal lowlands and then shipped off to her native state and crafted there at Bath into a fine and worthy sailing ship that then ran coastwise up and down the Atlantic till the hand of God recrafted and changed her in a moment, in the twinkling of His eye, into a mystery all insolvable, which He showed freely and for the merest asking, lest anyone take too much for granted his or her precarious grasp upon existence.

So what once was whole she saw now all in pieces, this Miriam Stover, this friend of captain and captain's daughter, and pieces of it she took, in two dimensions on photo negatives and, too, in her heart and mind, touched it even, touched these remnant timbers and found rough and unfinished that which certainly was finished, and in so doing all in all knew as much as anyone did of the *Deering's* last end. And then she put the camera on the car's front seat beside her, and took what of the old story she could and did have and started the long drive

The *Carroll A. Deering*'s capstan and timbers, Hatteras, N.C.

home to Maine, circling right back to where it all began, to the town of
Bath where once the shipwrights dwelled, beside a river that like all
rivers ran down to the stern mother and capricious lover of men—

The sea.

DOC MAURICE FOLB REMEMBERS
Hatteras Island, North Carolina
Summer 1973

The children of Cape Hatteras High School were concocting a
magazine, a recollective repository called *Seachest*, and among the old-
timers they sought out for good copy at their parents' suggestion was
the pharmacist's mate Doc Folb. Hadn't he been stationed at the cape

back in the Twenties? Might'n't he remember it all? Maybe he knew what happened way back yonder.

The old man who as a medic was the closest thing to a doctor Hatteras Island had during the time of their grandparents and great-grandparents did not disappoint them, for Doc Folb said:

> Yes, I was here when the *Carroll A. Deering* went on the point. I'm one of the survivors that actually saw the *Carroll A. Deering*. She went with all five masts; all sails set. When the Coast Guard went out to her they found the table set. They never found a man, a boat, or anything. . . . I believe that the men got in the quicksand—it was awful quicksandy out there.
>
> Never found any hide or hair, nor a boat or anything from her. Everything disappeared. The only survivor was a cat, I believe.

ON A CONTINENTAL SHELF
Ol' Store
Oriental, North Carolina
June 28–29, 1999

In a decommissioned general store in Oriental, North Carolina, now called the Ol' Store and overseen by two elderly fisherfolk, Billy and Lucille Truitt, among two dozen ship's models and small representations of Carolina's working watercraft, high on a shelf and at a central point in this reliquary shop (full of old toasters, haircurlers, dusty dolls, umbrellas so old they've been innocent of water for forty years if not sixty and whose original owners probably called them bumbershoots) sat a schooner model that Hunter Simpson, a young mariner just in from rounding Maw Point and boating up the Neuse and slamming a runabout into the river's southwesterly waves, focused upon and drifted through the dusty detritus to see up close, late one June afternoon.

There was the *Carroll A. Deering*, fully rigged with only the flying jib not set, just as the real *Deering* herself had been when she foundered on the Outer Diamond nearly eighty years earlier.

But this *was* the *Deering*, a part of her, there before the boy. The little ship that stood as icon of the larger had in real fact been carved and crafted from one of her timbers, brought home for that purpose by a one who long ago had stood at Hatteras and seen her, the real honest to God *her*, on the Diamond before she broke apart and fetched up in pieces upon the Outer Banks.

"Man that made that model, his name was Dameron Gray," said Lucille Truitt, who sat in an old easy chair with a chihuahua nearby and presided over the Ol' Store. "He was a barber over on Hatteras, and kind of a preacher, too—he'd bury folks and not charge their families. I headed shrimp one whole summer to get the money to pay for that little ship."

Then she shifted halfway round in her chair, which faced her west so that now she cast her gaze east-by-northeast, out of the store and across the little point of trees that was Oriental and down and past the baylike lower Neuse and across the oceanlike Pamlico Sound and on to the thin strip of seabeach from which the drifter, the pilgrim, the native alike can him- or herself gaze outward toward no other land at all. She was staring a long ways away at Cape Hatteras and Diamond Shoals.

"Don't you reckon it ought to go back over there to Hatteras?" Lucille Truitt asked, implored even, as if the reunification she might will and effect between her artifact and its place of creation might also suggest a reunion of the actual ship and her long-lost captain and crew, that we might know of them the intricacies of their great and lasting mystery before—in some perfect world where all wrecks are righted and all histories rectified—we sent them, restored, whole and hale and hearty, on their way to the Hampton Roads port-of-call they never made and, thence, sent a captain home to his family on the Fore River shore in Maine.

"That shipwreck museum they're gon be building over yonder at Hatteras village—don't you reckon it ought to be in there?" she asked again.

"*Don't you?*"

LOST
Diamond Shoals, North Carolina
January 30–31, 1921

On as nice and clear a winter's night as the Coast Guardsmen ashore could remember, and without warning or signal or cry of distress from sea to shore, the five-masted schooner *Carroll A. Deering* struck the southwest side of Outer Diamond Shoal. Wherever they were when she grounded, these were the men, and this the roll, of her crew:

Willis B. Wormell, Master
    61 Lawn Avenue, Portland, Maine
    Born September 16th, 1854
Charles McLellan, Mate
    Born about 1881–85
Johan Frederickson, Bo'sn
    Mobile, Alabama
    Naturalized American, from Finland
    Born October 15, 1872
James A. Benjamin, Steward
    92 Hammond Street, Boston, Massachusetts
    From French West Indies, born 1869
Herbert Pillsbury Bates, Engineer
    Islesboro, Maine, born February 15, 1887
Niels P. Nielsen, Able-Bodied Seaman
    40 South Street, New York City
    Of Arkies, Denmark, born May 3, 1896
Niels M. Olesen, A.B.
    25 South Street, New York City
    Of Denmark, born January 3, 1890
S. Christian Pedersen, A.B.
    Denmark, born 1894
Peter Sorensen, A.B.
    Denmark, born 1902

Alfred Jorgensen, A.B.
    Denmark, born 1896
Hans Charles Jensen, A.B.
    54 Commercial Place, Norfolk, Virginia
    Of Ikast, Jutland, Denmark
    Born September 6, 1900

These eleven men lost at sea—and what happened to them and what they did between Frying Pan Shoals and Lookout Shoals and Diamond Shoals the last week of January over eighty years ago and how they came to be so lost—were and are the mystery of the *Carroll A. Deering*. Until the Day of Judgment, that great day when the secrets of all hearts shall be known and the sea shall at long last give up her dead . . . *requiescat in pacem*.

Where last these men were seen and known to be, pelicans now go gliding low and slowly over the water, their long wet beaks glistening in the morning sun that plates the rolling ocean and makes its green waters go gold, and the grand brown birds fly like messengers to the nowadays from the back times before history, bearing memories of mariners so ancient that even the sea herself must work hard to recall them.

Among that antique, phantom crew, there is a preacher who sails the boundless sea, who regards all the wisdom and folly of humankind and always has, and who casts a cold eye upon all the living and the dead. The race is not to the swift, nor the battle to the strong, nor favor to men of skill—time and chance, saith the preacher, befall us all. Hear him, all ye nations. Hear ye.

Amen.

opposite: The schooner *Carroll A. Deering*

she sailed to her death...
with not a soul on board

THE CARROLL A. DEERING

Captain Merritt, the regular skipper, was put ashore at Lewes, Delaware, because of illness. Captain Wormell came out of retirement to take command. The schooner proceeded to a South American port and on the return voyage piled up off Hatteras, January 31, 1921, a total loss. An examination of the stranded vessel revealed all sails set, rigging secure, everything aboard in good order... *but not a trace of her boats or her captain and crew, her fate is still a mystery.*

The "Carroll A. Deering" was launched by G. G. Deering Company in 1919. She was the last of 28 five-masted schooners built at Bath, Maine. This was a sizeable ship, 2,114 gross tons, 255.1′ x 44.3′ x 25.3′. All her deck machinery was Hyde, for those famous old Deering ships were well-built, well-equipped and well-found.

That desire for nautical perfection is still alive here in Maine. While the change in ships from wood and wind to steel and steam has changed the machines we build, it has not changed our thinking. Into every Hyde windlass, winch and steering gear still goes the honest New England effort to give best to those who serve on the sea.

CHRONOLOGY

1833	October 18	Gardiner G. Deering born, Edgecomb, Maine.
1854	September 16	Willis Bradford Wormell born, Lubec, Maine.
1866		Deering and Donnell partner in shipbuilding firm.
1882	April 11	Carroll Atwood Deering born.
1884	September 6	Lula M. Wormell born, Lubec, Maine.
1886	April 12	Christopher Columbus Gray born, Avon, N.C.
		Deering and Donnell part ways, having built 70 vessels.
1905	May 6	G. G. Deering Company incorporates.
1914	December 5–6	*Alice M. Lawrence*, six-masted schooner, Willis Wormell, master, runs aground on Tuckernuck Shoal, Nantucket Sound, Mass.
	December 17	After salvage, Captain Wormell and crew abandon ship.
1918	August 14	German U-117 sinks five-masted schooner *Dorothy B. Barrett*, William M. Merritt, master, off Cape May, N.J.
	August 16	Mine laid by U-117 sinks British tanker *Mirlo* off Hatteras Island, N.C. Heroic rescue by John Allen Midgett's Chicamacomico station of U.S. Coast Guard.
1919	April 4	*Carroll A. Deering* is launched at G. G. Deering Company Yards, Washington Street, along the Kennebec River, Bath, Maine.
1920	July 19	*Deering* arrives at Newport News from Guayanilla, Puerto Rico.
	August 26	*Deering* sails from Hampton Roads, Va., loaded with coal.
	September 2	*Deering* stops at Lewes, Delaware; Captain Merritt requests replacement.

September 9		Captain Willis Wormell, the relief captain, and Charles McLellan, the new first mate, go aboard the *Deering* at Lewes, set sail for Rio de Janeiro, Brazil.
December 2		*Deering* sails light from Rio, bound for Hampton Roads, Va.
Christmastime		Mrs. Wormell hears from her husband that he is sailing home from Rio by way of Barbados with his most unruly crew ever.
1921	January	At Bridgetown, Barbados, First Mate McLellan threatens Wormell, is jailed. Captain Wormell gets McLellan released in time to sail.
	January 9	*Deering* clears Carlisle Bay, Bridgetown, Barbados.
	January 18	*Deering* is off Cape Canaveral on the Florida coast.
	January 20	SS *Hewitt*, hauling sulfur to Portland, Maine, clears Sabine, Tex.
		Deering is off Beaufort, S.C.
	January 23	*Deering* passes Frying Pan Light Vessel off Cape Fear, N.C., between 4 and 5 P.M.
	January 25	SS *Hewitt* last heard from, reportedly 250 miles north of Jupiter Inlet, Fla.
	January 29	*Carroll A. Deering* passes *Lookout Shoals Light Vessel No. 80* at 4:30 P.M., reports having lost both anchors and chains, asks to be reported, but lightship's wireless is out of commission. Steamship passing soon afterward ignores *LV 80*'s hail and steams away.
	January 30	*Deering* sails NNW and crosses shipping lanes near Hatteras, at 5:45 P.M., passing SS *Lake Elon* about twenty-five miles SW of Diamond Shoals light vessel. *Deering* sails onto Outer Diamond Shoals in the night.
	January 31	6:30 A.M. — Surfman C. P. Brady, on lookout at Cape Hatteras Coast Guard Station No. 183, sees a five-masted schooner on the shoals at dawn. 3:30 P.M. — surfmen of Station 183 notify Norfolk Division they

noticed a yawlboat missing from the schooner, but could not, due to heavy seas, come within a quarter-mile of the wreck and cannot identify it. No trace of schooner's crew.

February 1	Seas breaking over shipwreck's deck. Station 183 surfboat again fails to reach schooner. 1:30 P.M. — cutter *Seminole* at Diamond Shoals; Keeper B. B. Miller of Cape Hatteras Station and crew board *Seminole* to spend night.
February 2	*Seminole* steams toward schooner, puts Miller with surfboat and crew off as close as they all can get; Station 183 crew rebuffed again by the great waves. 1:25 P.M. — *Seminole* backs into 6½ fathoms, ¾ mi. from schooner, sees "neither life nor wreckage visible." *Seminole* boiler acts up and she stands for Wilmington.
February 4	Wrecker *Rescue*, of Norfolk, arrives Cape Hatteras 9:30 A.M. and approaches shipwreck with cutter *Manning*; schooner's identity is confirmed as *Carroll A. Deering*. At 10:20 A.M., *Rescue* Captain James Carlson boards the *Deering*, stays aboard with his men till 4:30 P.M.
Late February	*Deering* breaking up on Diamond Shoals. Bow section of hull drifts to Ocracoke Island and lodges in sand at shore.
March 15–16	*Seminole* tows, then dynamites, derelict *Deering*.
April 11	At Buxton, N.C., Christopher Columbus Gray reports finding note in bottle on the beach, purportedly written by someone on *Deering* and telling of *Deering*'s capture by pirates.
May 23–24	Handwriting of bottle message authenticated by Portland, Maine, experts as being that of *Deering* engineer Herbert Bates.
May 24	Schooner *Mary J. Haynie* wrecks, Pamlico Sound, near Ocracoke.

	Late May– early June	Lula Wormell, with Captain Merritt and Reverend Dr. Addison B. Lorimer of Central Square Baptist Church, Portland, go to Washington, D.C. Senator Hale of Maine helps them, introducing them to Secretary of Commerce Herbert Hoover, who places Lawrence Richey in charge of federal investigation.
	June 1	Schooner *Laura A. Barnes* wrecks at Bodie Island, N.C.
	June 2	"Proposed Instruction" from State Department to all American consular officers at seaports: "Make discreet inquiries and investigate carefully any clues which may lead to the discovery of the crew of the *Carroll A. Deering* and an explanation of the disaster."
	June 21–22	Story of *Deering* investigation breaks, along with word of the vanished fleet, causing immediate alarm and panic in international shipping circles.
	August 1–3	Federal handwriting experts certify that Christopher C. Gray is true author of fraudulent bottle message.
	August 18–21	Lawrence Richey travels from Norfolk to Cape Hatteras aboard lighthouse tender *Columbine*, at Hatteras Light interrogates Gray, who confesses to his hoax.
	August 25	In Washington, Richey announces the bottle-message hoax.
1922		Gardiner G. "Gard" Deering dies in Bath, Maine, three years after building and launching the *Carroll A. Deering*.
	October 30	In New York, attorney F. L. Allen files for Captain Wormell's life insurance; Lula Wormell and her mother have given Willis Wormell up for dead.
1935	September 3	In Maine, Lula Wormell, now of Buffalo, N.Y., marries Leon J. Cabana, also of Buffalo.
1948	May–June	Writer Edward Rowe Snow visits Lula Wormell Cabana in Buffalo, N.Y.; Captain William Merritt in South Portland, Maine; and Carroll A. Deering in Bath, Maine. Latter rings the *Deering*'s bell.
1952	February 5	Christopher Columbus Gray dies, Buxton, N.C.

1955	September 19	Hurricane Ione hits Outer Banks, floats the bow section of the *Carroll A. Deering* nine miles, from Ocracoke to Hatteras Island.
1967	March 12	Carroll Atwood Deering dies, Georgetown, Maine.
1975	October	Lula Wormell Cabana dies, Buffalo, N.Y. Whereabouts of *Carroll A. Deering*'s ocean chart unknown.

FROM THE DECK LOGS OF THE LIGHT VESSELS AT FRYING PAN SHOALS, LOOKOUT SHOALS, AND DIAMOND SHOALS, JANUARY 23–31, 1921

Logs record date and time, sea conditions, wind direction and speed (mph), weather, barometric pressure (inches of mercury), and temperature (Farenheit).

Date/Time	Frying Pan Shoals	Lookout Shoals	Diamond Shoals
Sunday, January 23			
6 A.M.	Smooth, WSW 13–18, clear 30.30", 56°		Smooth, W 13–18, cloudy 30.06", 62°
Noon	Smooth, W 13–18 clear, 30.24", 58°		Smooth, W 18–23 clear, 29.99", 64°
6 P.M.	Smooth, WSW 13–18, clear 30.14", 58°		Smooth, WSW 18–23, clear, 29.92", 65°
Midnight	Unchanged since 6 P.M.		Moderate seas, NW 13–18, cloudy, 29.95", 58°
Monday, January 24			
6 A.M.	Choppy, NNE 18–23, cloudy, 30.18", 56°		Moderate, N 18–23, cloudy, 29.98", 54°
Noon	Light roll, NE 13–18, cloudy, 30.20", 56°		Moderate, N 13–18, cloudy, 30.08", 58°
6 P.M.	Smooth, SW 8–13, clear, 30.14", 56°		Smooth, N 3–8, clear, 30.04", 59°

Date/Time	Frying Pan Shoals	Lookout Shoals	Diamond Shoals
Midnight	Smooth, W 8–13, clear, 30.18", 52°		Moderate, N 18–23, clear, 30.10", 49°

Tuesday, January 25th

	Frying Pan Shoals	Lookout Shoals	Diamond Shoals
6 A.M.	Choppy, NE 18–23, clear, 30.30", 48°	Choppy, NE 25, partly cloudy, 30.25", 48°	Rough, N 28–34, clear, 30.16", 43°
Noon	Choppy, NE 23–28, clear, 30.36", 58°	Choppy, NE 20, cloudy, 30.30", 45°	Rough, N 34–40, clear, 30.26", 42°
6 P.M.	Choppy, NE 23–28, cloudy, 30.44", 54°	Choppy, NE 20, cloudy, 30.30", 43°	Moderate, N 28–34, clear, 30.28", 41°
Midnight	Choppy, NE 23–28, cloudy, —, 48°	Choppy, NE 20, misty, 30.30", 38°	Moderate, N 28–34, cloudy, 30.28", 39°

Wednesday, January 26

	Frying Pan Shoals	Lookout Shoals	Diamond Shoals
6 A.M.	Rough, NE 28–34, light rain, 30.40", 46°	Very rough, NE 30, mists, 30.38", 36°	Moderate, N 23–28, cloudy, 30.28", 39°
Noon	Rough, NE 40–48, light rain, mist, 30.40", 48°	Very rough, NE 35, fog, 30.35", 35°	Moderate, NNE 28–34, cloudy, 30.30", 40°
6 P.M.	Rough, ENE 40–48, light rain, mist, 30.20", 54°	Very rough, NE 40, rain, 30.30", 35°	Moderate, NNE 28–34, rain, 30.23", 45°
Midnight	Rough, SE 48–56, rain, mist, 30.04", 54°	Very rough, E 45, rain, 30.10", 60°	Choppy, E 28–34, rain, 30.16", 48°

Date/Time	Frying Pan Shoals	Lookout Shoals	Diamond Shoals
Thursday, January 27th			
6 A.M.	Rough, ESE 18–23, cloudy, 29.88", 52°	Seas very large, breaking over lightship, ESE 45, rain, 29.98", 61°	Rough, E 34–40, rain, 30.00", 52°
Noon	Rough, NE 56–65	Seas breaking over ship, NE 50, fog and mist, 29.90", 62°	Rough, ENE 48–56, rain, 29.86", 60°
6 P.M.	Same as noon	Seas breaking continuously over ship, NE 50, fog and mist, 29.83", 60°	Rough, ENE 48–56, rain, 29.85", 61°
Midnight	Rough, NE 56–65, 30.00"	Seas very large, breaking over ship, NE 75, fog and mist, 29.89", 46°	Rough, N 48–56, misty, 29.84", 59°
Friday, January 28th			
6 A.M.	Rough, NNE 48–56, cloudy, 30.12", 46°	Very rough, NE 50, cloudy, 29.96", 46°	Rough, N 48–56, misty, 29.80", 50°
Noon	Rough, NNE 40–48, clear, 30.20", 54°	Very rough, NE 45, cloudy, 30.00", 52°	Rough, N 40–48, cloudy, 29.95", 52°
6 P.M.	Rough, N 28–34, clear, 30.24", 48°	Rough, NE 35, cloudy, 30.08", 52°	Rough, N 40–48, cloudy, 30.01", 50°

Date/Time	Frying Pan Shoals	Lookout Shoals	Diamond Shoals
Midnight	Rough, N 23–28, clear, 30.30", 48°	Rough, NE 35, cloudy, 30.15", 50°	Moderate swell, N 18–23, clear, 30.04", 48°

Saturday, January 29th

Date/Time	Frying Pan Shoals	Lookout Shoals	Diamond Shoals
6 A.M.	Rough, N 23–28, overcast, 30.30", 46°	Rough and lumpy, NE 25, hazy, 30.18", 52°	Moderate swell, N 13–18, clear, 30.04", 48°
Noon	Easterly roll, NNE 13–18, hazy, 30.34", 50°	Rough and lumpy, N 10, foggy, 30.20", 54°	Moderate swell, NNW 13–18, clear, 30.10", 54°
6 P.M.	Easterly roll, SE 8–13, cloudy, 30.30", 48°	Moderate smooth, SSW calm, hazy, 30.20", 54°	Moderate swell, N 8–13, cloudy, 30.08", 56°
Midnight	Easterly roll, NW 8–13, clear, 30.24", 50°	Moderate smooth, NW 4, clear, 30.15", 52°	Moderate swell, NW 3–8, cloudy, 30.08", 55°

Sunday, January 30th

Date/Time	Frying Pan Shoals	Lookout Shoals	Diamond Shoals
6 A.M.	Easterly roll, calm, clear, 30.24", 50°	Moderate smooth, NW 4, clear, 30.15", 52°	Moderate swell, NW 3–8, cloudy 30.01", 52°
Noon	Easterly roll, SSW 3–8, clear, 30.24", 60°	Moderate smooth, NW 4, clear, 30.10", 58°	Moderate swell, WNW 3–8, hail, 29.98", 60°
6 P.M.	Moderate smooth, SW 13–18, clear, 30.10", 56°	Moderate smooth, SW 6, cloudy, 30.08", 58°	Moderate swell, WSW 3–8, clear, 29.90", 58°
Midnight	Moderate smooth, SW 13–18, cloudy, 30.10", 54°	Moderate smooth, SW 8, hazy, 30.00", 56°	Smooth, SW 13–18, cloudy, 29.86", 57°

Date/Time	Frying Pan Shoals	Lookout Shoals	Diamond Shoals

Monday, January 31st

6 A.M.	Choppy, SW 13–18, cloudy, 30.10", 54°		Smooth, SW 13–18, cloudy, 29.83", 59°
Noon	Moderate smooth, W 13–18, clear, 30.16", 56°		Smooth, W 18–23, clear, 29.91", 58°
6 P.M.	WNW 8–13, clear, 30.16", 54°		Smooth, N 23–28, clear, 29.98", 53°
Midnight	Choppy, NNW 18–23, clear, 30.30", 50°		Smooth, N 23–28, hail, 30.06", 50°

ACKNOWLEDGMENTS

All of us lucky enough to grow up trekking to the Outer Banks of North Carolina heard stories of shoals and shipwrecks from earliest childhood, a favorite being the tale of the fabled ghost ship *Carroll A. Deering*. Short versions of the *Deering*'s story appear in John Harden's *The Devil's Tramping Ground and Other North Carolina Mystery Stories*; Judge Charles Harry Whedbee's *Legends of the Outer Banks and Tar Heel Tidewater*; Edward Rowe Snow's *Mysteries and Adventures along the Atlantic Coast*; and David Stick's *Graveyard of the Atlantic*. Ormonde De Kay Jr.'s account is in *Mysteries of the Deep*, edited by Joseph J. Thorndike Jr.

Many people have helped me enormously as I sought to detail the ghost ship's life and times. Brian Edwards of the Outer Banks History Center in Manteo, North Carolina, sent me historical, photographic, and cartographic materials of all kinds, along with his excellent article "A Brief History of Prohibition in Northeastern North Carolina," from *Tributaries*, a publication of the North Carolina Maritime History Council (October 1999)—a fascinating window on the era and region where the *Deering* was lost. Wynne Dough, also of the OBHC, provided me with the *Report of Assistance Rendered* from January 31 and February 4, 1921, for Coast Guard Stations 182, 183, 184, and 186 (Big Kinnakeet, Cape Hatteras, Creed's Hill, and Hatteras Inlet); Nathan Hilkert of the National Archives, East Point, Georgia, sent me the log entries of those same stations for that fateful week. From the heart of the schooner world has come clear and steady information and advice from Nathan Lipfert, library director, his assistants Cathy Matero and Ren Lamphere, and Anne Witty, curator, all of the Maine Maritime Museum, Bath, Maine. Here at home, Bob Anthony, curator, and Alice Cotten, reference historian, of the North Carolina Collection, and Jerry Cotten, photographic archivist, and his assistant Keith Longiotti, Wilson Library, UNC–Chapel Hill, have always been sources of accuracy, aid, and comfort.

A key memo from Internet Public Library volunteer librarian Kristen Truong, School of Information, University of Michigan, Ann Arbor, led me directly to hundreds of pages concerning the *Carroll A. Deering* in the Lawrence Richey Papers at the Herbert Hoover Library, West Branch, Iowa, where archivists Cindy Worrell,

J. Patrick Wildenberg, and Jim E. Detlefsen have been extraordinary in their assistance to me. The Richey Papers included numerous FBI reports, handwriting analyses, correspondence between Richey and Lula Wormell, the Christopher Columbus Gray letters, early 1921 deck logs from the Carolina coastal lightships, and much illustrative material. At the National Archives, Pennsylvania Avenue, Washington, D.C., were the log of the U.S. Coast Guard Cutter *Seminole* (RG 26, Box 2068); records of the U.S. Coast Guard, *General Correspondence 1910–41* (RG 26, File 651, Box 1555), and Records of the Department of Commerce, Bureau of Lighthouses, *Correspondence 1911–39* (RG 26, File 80-E, Box 86), and Bureau of Marine Inspection and Navigation, *Correspondence 1884–1934* (RG 41, File 122229N, Box 2035).

Our American press spent a great deal of ink on the story of the *Deering*'s shipwreck and ensuing investigation, and my narrative owes much to newspapers of the day, including: the *Independent* and the *Daily Advance*, both of Elizabeth City, North Carolina; the *Portland Evening Express and Daily Advertiser*, Portland, Maine; the *Bath Daily Times*, Bath, Maine; the *Ledger-Dispatch*, Norfolk, Virginia; the *Washington Post*, the *Washington Times* (where Lula Wormell's *Six Points* ran), the *Washington Herald*, the *New York Times*, and the *Wall Street Journal*.

Personal recollections in this book were drawn from: M. B. "Doc" Folb, "We Call Him Doc," *Seachest* 1 (Summer 1973), and Folb's own "Reminiscences of Isolated Duty at Cape Hatteras," *U.S. Naval Medical Bulletin*, Supplement, 11, no. 4 (October 1927); Bosun Charles Peele, in William Keith Saunders's article "The *Carroll M. Deering*" [*sic*] in *The State* (February 25, 1939); Captain William Merritt, in Edward Snow's *Mysteries*; and Miriam Stover Thomas, in her piece "The Mystery of the *Carroll A. Deering*," *Downeast* (July 1972).

Works essential to sounding the coasts and maritime life of Maine and Carolina include David Stick's *The Outer Banks of North Carolina*; David Cecelski's *A Historian's Coast*; Captain Francis F. "Biff" Bowker's *Atlantic Four-Master: The Story of the Schooner "Herbert L. Rawding"*; Ralph Linwood Snow's and Captain Douglas K. Lee's *A Shipyard in Maine: Percy & Small and the Great Schooners*; Frederick F. Kaiser's *Built on Honor, Sailed with Skill: The American Coasting Schooner*; William Avery Baker's *A Maritime History of Bath, Maine, and the Kennebec River Region*; Richard L. Chenery III's *Old Coast Guard Stations, Vol. Two, North Carolina*; Ben Dixon MacNeill's *The Hatterasman*; Jan DeBlieu's *Hatteras Journal*; Sonny Williamson's *Unsung Heroes of the Surf: The Lifesaving Services of Carteret County*; Rodney Barfield's *Seasoned by Salt*; and Jay Barnes's *North Carolina's Hurricane History*.

Others who lent me a hand were: Julie Howard, director, Ocracoke Preservation Society, Ocracoke, N.C.; E. Michael DiPaolo, curator, and George Elliott of the Lewes Historical Society, Lewes, Delaware; Kathleen Barry, periodicals, Portland Public Library, Portland, Maine; Carolle Morini, photographic collections archivist, Marc M. Teatum, director of photographic services and images, Heather Shanks, photographic services coordinator, all of Peabody Essex Museum, Salem, Mass.; Don Pendergraft, Museum of the Albemarle, Elizabeth City, N.C.; Connie Mason, North Carolina Maritime Museum, Beaufort, N.C.; Mystic Seaport Library, Mystic, Conn.; Stephanie Philbrick, Shirley Grange, and Bill Barry, Center for Maine History, Maine Historical Society, Portland, Maine; Pauline J. Byrd, Islesboro Historical Society, Islesboro, Maine; James H. Mitchell, Islesboro, Maine; Dave Hackett, Harpswell Historical Society, Harpswell, Maine; Scott T. Price, historian, U.S. Coast Guard, Washington, D.C.; Debra Aaronson Lawless, Providence, R.I.; Everett E. Wallace, Brunswick, Maine; Henry Taylor, Brunswick, Maine; Max C. Chapman Jr., Scarborough, N.Y.; James Broughton, Washington, D.C.; Professor Bobbi Owen, Department of Dramatic Art, UNC–Chapel Hill; Joseph Schwartzer, director, Graveyard of the Atlantic Museum, Hatteras, N.C.; and Lucille and Billy Truitt, Ol' Store, Oriental, N.C.

For generously sharing family information and materials, I give great thanks to Stuart Gillard Stearns of Chatham, Mass., grand-nephew of Captain Wormell; to Patrick R. Davis of Tifton, Ga., great-grandson of Carroll A. Deering, and to his mother Anne Davis and his uncle Pat Moffat, granddaughter and grandson of Mr. Deering; and to kinswoman Camelia Deering Buffam, Panama City, Fla.

University of North Carolina Press editor-in-chief David Perry, ever adventurous, wanted the *Deering's* story told anew from the moment I proposed it, and helping this come to pass have been his assistant Mark Simpson-Vos, project editor Pam Upton, design director Rich Hendel, cartographer Heidi Perov, marketing manager Kathy Ketterman, and many, many others at this venerable, wonderful publishing house, not the least of which has been its director, Kate Torrey. My UNC–Chapel Hill Creative Writing Program colleagues, particularly director Marianne Gingher, have been steadfastly encouraging. Department of English chair James Thompson granted me Kenan travel funds for research in the state of Maine; former chair William Andrews, having nominated me for a Chapman Family Fellowship, granted me a research leave and assigned me a tireless research assistant in outdoorsman Bryan Giemza. As a Chapman Fellow, I began this book at the Institute of Arts and Humanities, where director Ruel Tyson welcomed me into a terrific group of seminarians.

Three great friends who stared with me into what Dylan called "the foggy ruins of time" and tried to cipher this great mystery—often on the waters of the Carolina east—were my longtime musical and nautical partner Jack Herrick of the Red Clay Ramblers, incomparable historian David Cecelski, and Roanoke-Chowan poet Michael McFee.

Jerry Leath Mills once more turned his considerable intellect, energy, and attention to a manuscript of mine, which profited greatly from the careful eye of this peerless teacher and editor, this dearest of friends.

Between them, my late father, Martin Bland Simpson Jr., Lieutenant JG, USN, and my late uncle, Charles A. Lamborn, Commander, USN, gave me my first awareness of men and great ships.

To all these people I offer my deepest gratitude, to all the living and the dead.

MBS III

ILLUSTRATION CREDITS